A CourseGuide for

Basics of Biblical Greek

William D. Mounce

ZONDERVAN ACADEMIC

A CourseGuide for Basics of Biblical Greek

Copyright © 2019 by William Mounce

ISBN 978-0-310-11108-5 (softcover)

Requests for information should be addressed to:
Zondervan, 3900 Sparks Dr. SE, Grand Rapids, Michigan 49546

All Scripture quotations, unless otherwise indicated, are taken from The Holy Bible, New International Version®, NIV®. Copyright © 1973, 1978, 1984, 2011 by Biblica, Inc.® Used by permission of Zondervan. All rights reserved worldwide. www.Zondervan.com. The "NIV" and "New International Version" are trademarks registered in the United States Patent and Trademark Office by Biblica, Inc.®

Any internet addresses (websites, blogs, etc.) and telephone numbers in this book are offered as a resource. They are not intended in any way to be or imply an endorsement by Zondervan, nor does Zondervan vouch for the content of these sites and numbers for the life of this book.

No part of this publication may be reproduced, stored in a retrieval system, or transmitted in any form or by any means—electronic, mechanical, photocopy, recording, or any other—except for brief quotations in printed reviews, without the prior permission of the publisher.

Printed in the United States of America

CONTENTS

Introduction 5

1-2. The Greek Language and Learning Greek 7

3. The Alphabet and Pronunciation 11

4. Punctuation and Syllabification 15

5. Introduction to English Nouns 18

6. Nominative and Accusative; Article 21

7. Genitive and Dative 25

8. Prepositions and εἰμί 28

9. Adjectives 31

10. Third Declension 35

11. First and Second Person; Personal Pronouns 38

12. αὐτός 42

13. Demonstrative Pronouns and Adjectives οὗτος, ἐκεῖνος 46

14. Relative Pronoun 50

15. Introduction to Verbs 54

16. Present Active Indicative 57

17. Contract Verbs 61

18. Present Middle/Passive Indicative 65

19. **Future Active and Middle Indicative** 69

20. **Verbal Roots (Patterns 2-4)** 72

21. **Imperfect Indicative** 76

22. **Second Aorist Active and Middle Indicative** 79

23. **First Aorist Active and Middle Indicative** 83

24. **Aorist and Future Passive Indicative** 87

25. **Perfect Indicative** 90

26. **Introduction to Participles** 94

27. **Imperfect (Present) Adverbial Participles)** 97

28. **Perfect (Aorist) Adverbial Participles** 100

29. **Adjectival Participles** 103

30. **Combinative (Perfect) Participles and Genitive Absolutes** 107

31. **Subjunctive** 111

32. **Infinitive** 115

33. **Imperative** 118

34. **Indicative of δίδωμι** 122

35. **Nonindicative of δίδωμι and Conditional Sentences** 125

36. **ἴστημι, τίθημι, δείκνυμι, and Odds 'n Ends** 129

Introduction

Welcome to *A CourseGuide for Basics of Biblical Greek*. These guides were created for formal and informal students alike who want to engage deeper in biblical, theological, or ministry studies. We hope this guide will provide an opportunity for you to grow not only in your understanding, but also in your faith.

How to Use this Guide

This guide is meant to be used in conjunction with the book *Basics of Biblical Greek Grammar* and its corresponding videos, *Basics of Biblical Greek Video Lectures*. After you have read each chapter in the book and watched the accompanying video lesson, the materials in this guide will help you review and assess what you have learned. Application-oriented questions are included as well. For additional practice, you will want to complete exercises found in *Basics of Biblical Greek Workbook*.

Each CourseGuide has been individually designed to best equip you in your studies, but in general, you can expect the following components. Most CourseGuides begin every chapter with a "You Should Know" section, which highlights key terminology, people, and facts to remember. This section serves as a helpful summary for directing your studies. Reflection questions, typically two to three per chapter, prompt you to summarize key points you've learned. Discussion questions invite you to an even deeper level of engagement. Finally, most chapters will end with a short quiz to test your retention. You can find the answer key to each quiz at the bottom of the page following it.

For Further Study

CourseGuides accompany books and videos from some of the world's top biblical and theological scholars. They may be used independently, or in small groups or classrooms, offering quality instruction to equip students for academic and ministry pursuits. If you would like to engage in further study with Zondervan's CourseGuides, the full lineup may be viewed online. After completing your studies with *A CourseGuide for Basics of Biblical Greek*, we recommend moving on to *A CourseGuide for Greek Grammar Beyond the Basics* and *A CourseGuide for Basics of Biblical Hebrew*.

CHAPTERS 1 AND 2

The Greek Language and Learning Greek

You Should Know

- The Greek language has a long and rich history stretching all the way from the fourteenth century BC to the present.

- As the Greek language spread across the world and met other languages, it was altered (which is true of any language). The dialects also interacted with each other. Eventually this adaptation resulted in what today we call Koine Greek (or more inexactly, "biblical Greek"). "Koine" means "common" (from the phrase κοινὴ διάλεκτος, the "common language") and describes the common, everyday form of the language used by everyday people.

- The Koine period lasted until the fourth century, which saw the rise of Byzantium, whose name was changed to Constantinople and eventually Istanbul. Byzantium Greek describes the language until 1453 when Constantinople was conquered by the Ottoman Turks, and from that date until now we call the language Modern Greek.

- For a long time Koine Greek confused scholars because it was significantly different from Classical Greek. Some hypothesized that it was a combination of Greek, Hebrew, and Aramaic. Others attempted to explain it as a "Holy Ghost language," meaning that God created a special language just for the Bible. But discoveries of Greek papyri found in Egypt over the past one hundred years have shown that this language was the language of the everyday people, used in the writings of wills, private letters, receipts, shopping lists, etc.

- Make flash cards for vocabulary words and word endings—3 x 5 index cards cut in thirds are a nice size. You can put them in your pocket and take them anywhere. Use them while waiting in lines, during work breaks, before classes, etc. You can also purchase *Basics of Biblical Greek Vocabulary Cards* (Zondervan), or you can purchase a vocabulary app for your phone.

- When memorizing words, use mnemonic devices. For example, the Greek word for "face" is transliterated as *prosōpon*, so it could be remembered by the phrase, "pour soap on my face." It seems that the sillier these devices are the better, so don't be ashamed.

- You must pronounce Greek consistently and write it neatly. If your pronunciation varies, it is difficult to remember the words.

- The greatest motivation for learning Greek comes during the homework assignments. Because most of the exercises are drawn from the New Testament, you are constantly reminded why you are learning the language.

- Very few people can "pick up" a language. For most of us it takes time, lots of it. Plan for that; remind yourself what you are trying to do, and spend the necessary time. But along with the amount of time is the matter of consistency. Spend time every day; getting to know the language of the New Testament deserves at least that. Remember, "Those who cram, perish."

- Discipline is the bottom line. There are no magical solutions to learning Greek. It is achievable if you want it. It comes at a cost, but the rewards are tremendous.

Quiz

1. (T/F) The earlier form of the Greek language is called "Linear B."

2. (T/F) The style of Greek used by writers from the time of Homer through Plato is called "Archaic Greek."

3. What is the style of Greek which spread throughout the Hellenist world after Alexander the Great?

a) Doric
b) Koine
c) Ionic
d) Attic

4. Byzantium Greek describes the language of Greece during which of the following periods?

   a) The Hellenistic Age of Alexander the Great
   b) From the time of King Philip of Macedonia until the fourth century
   c) From the fourth century until Constantinople was conquered by the Ottoman Turks
   d) From the conquering of Constantinople in 1453 until the present time

5. (T/F) The study of Greek papyri confirms that the Greek of the New Testament was the "common language" of the first century.

6. Which of the following are considered Romance languages?

   a) Latin
   b) English
   c) Greek
   d) Sanskrit
   e) All of the above
   f) None of the above

7. What is the hypothetical base language group that later developed into four language groups?

   a) Proto-Germanic
   b) Semitic
   c) Proto-Indo-European
   d) Linear B

8. The main purpose of learning Greek is:

   a) To illustrate theological points
   b) To communicate more clearly the Word of God
   c) To discover what the New Testament "really says"
   d) To develop critical thinking skills

9. (T/F) The only way to be a good preacher is to know Greek.

10. Which of the following is imperative to learning a language?
   a) Recognition
   b) Repetition
   c) Memorization
   d) Transliteration

ANSWER KEY
1. T, 2. F, 3. B, 4. C, 5. T, 6. A, 7. C, 8. B, 9. F, 10. C

CHAPTER 3

The Alphabet and Pronunciation

You Should Know

- Which Greek lowercase letter is the 'ch' sound?
  – χ

- Which Greek lowercase letter is the 'a' sound?
  – α

- Which Greek lowercase letter is the 'z' sound?
  – ζ

- The Greek letter κ makes which sound?
  – 'k'

- The Greek letter ρ makes which sound?
  – 'r'

- The Greek letter δ makes which sound?
  – 'd'

- It is essential that you learn the Greek alphabet right away. You cannot learn anything else until you do.

- Learn the English name, how to write the small letter, and how to pronounce the letter.

- The vowels in Greek are α, ε, η, ι, ο, υ, and ω.

- Every word beginning with a vowel must have either a rough or smooth breathing mark. If the word begins with a diphthong, the breathing mark is over the second vowel. If the word begins with a single vowel and is capitalized, the breathing mark goes before the first vowel.

- A diphthong consists of two vowels pronounced as a single sound. The second vowel is always an ι or υ.

- An improper diphthong is a diphthong with an iota subscript under the first vowel. The iota subscript does not affect pronunciation but is important in translation.

Quiz

1. How many letters are there in the Greek alphabet?
    a) 16
    b) 22
    c) 24
    d) 32

2. What is transliteration?
    a) The equivalent of a letter in another language
    b) A similar combination of letters in one language has the same meaning as the same combination in another
    c) The letters or words that can be used interchangeably within various languages
    d) All of the above

3. Which of the following letters is classified as a "nasal"?
    a) Eta-η
    b) Nu-ν
    c) Sigma-σ
    d) Omicron-o
    e) All of the above

4. What is a diphthong?
    a) A combination of two consonants that produce one sound
    b) A combination of two vowels that produce one sound

c) A combination of a vowel and a consonant that produces one sound

d) A combination of three or more letters that produces one sound

5. What is the small iota written under certain vowels called?
   a) An iota diphthong
   b) A furtive iota
   c) An iota subscript
   d) Diaeresis

6. What is placed over a diphthong to indicate the letters ought to be pronounced separately? (The two dots in the word Ἠσαΐας, for example).
   a) Crasis
   b) Diaeresis
   c) Elision
   d) Rough Breathing Mark

7. Which of the following is not a vowel?
   a) α
   b) η
   c) τ
   d) ο

8. How should you pronounce two gammas (γγ)?
   a) Like the gg in "eggs"
   b) Like the ng in "angel"
   c) Like the letters "gly"
   d) Like a single "g"

9. Which of the following is true of an iota subscript?
   a) It is a small ι written under the vowels α, η, or ω
   b) It is normally the last letter in a word
   c) It has no effect on the pronunciation
   d) It is essential for translation
   e) All of the above

10. Which Greek letter has two forms, one written only at the end of words?
   a) Beta
   b) Theta
   c) Xi
   d) Sigma

ANSWER KEY
1. C, 2. A, 3. B, 4. B, 5. C, 6. B, 7. C, 8. B, 9. E, 10. D

CHAPTER 4

Punctuation and Syllabification

You Should Know

- The word for "glory" is:
  – δόξα

- The word for "voice" is:
  – φωνή

- What is the best translation for the word γραφή?
  – Writing

- What is the best translation for the word ζωή?
  – Life

- What is the best translation for the word προφήτης?
  – Prophet

- The word for "world" is:
  – κόσμος

- A period above the line is a Greek semicolon, and an English semicolon is a Greek question mark. Periods and commas look the same.

- There are three accents. You do not have to know why they occur where they do, but place stress on the accented syllable.

- The **acute** accent shows that the pitch originally went up a little on the accented syllable (θάνατος).

- The **grave** accent shows that the voice originally dropped a little on the accented syllable (διὰ πύλης). When citing a single word that in the text has a grave, it is customary to change the grave to an acute. For example, if the sentence has διὰ πύλης and you want to reference the first word, you would write διά.

- The **circumflex** accent shows that the voice rose and then dropped a little on the accented syllable (γλῶσσα).

- English syllabification basically follows Greek syllabification. Listen to your teacher pronounce the words and it should become automatic.

- Memorizing vocabulary is one of the essential elements if you are going to enjoy the language.

Quiz

1. How many accents are there in the Greek language?
    a) 0
    b) 2
    c) 3
    d) 4

2. Which of the following symbols is used for a question mark in Greek:
    a) !
    b) ;
    c) *
    d) ,

3. An apostrophe is used when a final vowel is omitted from a Greek word. This omission is called:
    a) Crasis
    b) Diaeresis
    c) Elision
    d) Metathesis

4. Which of the following letters has an acute accent?
    a) λόγος
    b) καὶ
    c) ἀρχῇ
    d) None of the above

Punctuation and Syllabification | 17

5. Which of the following letters has a grave accent?

   a) λόγος
   b) καὶ
   c) ἀρχῇ
   d) None of the above

6. Which of the following letters has a circumflex accent?

   a) λόγος
   b) καὶ
   c) ἀρχῇ
   d) None of the above

7. Accents serve us very well in the area(s) of:

   a) Pronunciation
   b) Memorization
   c) Identification
   d) All of the above

8. How many words occur fifty times or more in the New Testament?

   a) 175
   b) 313
   c) 319
   d) 2,000
   e) 9,162

9. (T/F) Compound words are divided into syllables between the two words.

10. (T/F) In Greek there are no silent consonants so the π is always pronounced (as in πνεῦμα, "spirit").

ANSWER KEY
1. C, 2. B, 3. C, 4. A, 5. B, 6. C, 7. D, 8. B, 9. T, 10. T

CHAPTER 5

Introduction to English Nouns

You Should Know

- A definite article is:
  - "The"
- The indefinite article is:
  - "A"
- The verb γράφει can mean:
  - "he writes," "she writes," or "it writes."
- A noun is a word that stands for someone or something. In the sentence, "Bill threw his big black book at the strange teacher," the words "Bill," "book," and "teacher" are nouns.
- An adjective is a word that modifies a noun (or another adjective). In the sentence above, "big," "black," and "strange" are adjectives that modify nouns. In the sentence, "The dark brown Bible costs too much," "dark" is an adjective modifying the adjective "brown."
- A preposition is a word that shows the relationship between two items. For example, the relationship can be spatial ("The Greek text is *under* the bed") or temporal ("The student always studies *after* the ball game").
- A sentence can be broken down into two parts. The term subject describes the subject of the verb and what modifies the subject. Predicate describes the rest of the sentence, including the verb, direct object, etc.

- The definite article is the word "the." In the sentence, "The student is going to pass," the definite article is identifying one student in particular—not just any student, but *the* student.
- The indefinite article is the word "a." In the sentence, "A good student works every day on her Greek," the article is indefinite because it does not identify any one particular student. It is indefinite about the person of whom it is speaking.

Quiz

1. (T/F) You do not need to know English grammar in order to learn Greek grammar.

2. A declension is:
    a) A pattern of inflection
    b) A word that takes on the gender of the object it represents
    c) A word that is directly affected by the action of the verb
    d) A word that shows possession

3. Which of the following describes the rest of a sentence, including the verb, direct object, etc.?
    a) The subject
    b) The predicate
    c) The preposition
    d) The object

4. When a word changes its form because of its use in a sentence (from "she" to "her"), it is called:
    a) Case
    b) Inflection
    c) Subjective
    d) Adjective

5. Case refers to:
    a) The function of a word in the sentence
    b) The use of a word to describe an action

c) The omission of a word from a clause
  d) The use of a pronoun

6. An adjective:
   a) Modifies a verb
   b) Modifies a noun
   c) Is used for the direct object
   d) Introduces a dependent clause

7. An adverb:
   a) Modifies a verb
   b) Modifies a noun
   c) Is used for the direct object
   d) Introduces a dependent clause

8. What is a preposition?
   a) A word which modifies a verb
   b) A word which shows the relationship between two other items
   c) A word which is always the subject of the sentence
   d) A word which never takes an accent

9. The direct object:
   a) Describes the verb
   b) Is the person or thing directly affected by the verb
   c) Is the subject of the verb
   d) Is the purpose for the action of the verb

10. A prepositional phrase includes:
    a) The preposition
    b) The object
    c) Modifiers
    d) All of the above
    e) A & B

ANSWER KEY

1. F, 2. A, 3. B, 4. B, 5. A, 6. B, 7. A, 8. B, 9. B, 10. D

CHAPTER 6

Nominative and Accusative; Article

You Should Know

- What is the best translation for the word ἀγάπη, -ης, ἡ?
  - Love

- What is the best translation for the word ὥρα, -ας, ἡ?
  - Hour, occasion

- What is the best translation for the word βασιλεία, -ας, ἡ?
  - Kingdom

- What is the best translation for the word ἔργον, -ου, τό?
  - Work, deed

- What is the best translation for the word νῦν?
  - Now

- What is the best translation for the word δέ?
  - But

- What is the best translation for the word καιρός, -οῦ, ὁ?
  - Time

- What is the best translation for the word αὐτός, -ή, -ό?
  - He, she, it, they

- Greek uses different case endings to indicate the case (nominative; accusative), gender (masculine; feminine; neuter), and number (singular; plural).

- The stem of the word is the basic form of the word that carries its meaning. It is discovered by removing the case ending.

- Stems ending in an α or η are in the first declension; stems ending in ο are in the second declension.

- If a word is the subject of a verb, it is in the nominative case and uses nominative case endings. If a word is the direct object of a verb, it is in the accusative case and uses accusative case endings.

- Word order does not determine the function of a word. Normal Greek order is verb, subject, direct object, often with an initial conjunction. The lexical form of a noun is the nominative singular.

- These are the first three of the famous eight noun rules. Memorize them precisely:

    i. stems ending in α or η are in the first declension, stems ending in ο are in the second, and consonantal stems are in the third;
    ii. every neuter word has the same form in the nominative and accusative;
    iii. almost all neuter words end in α in the nominative and accusative plural.

- The definite article is the only article in Greek. There is no indefinite article ("a," cf. 6.28). For this reason you can refer to the Greek definite article simply as the article.

Quiz

1. Nouns that have stems ending in ο are:
    a) First declension
    b) Second declension
    c) Third declension

2. Nouns that have stems ending in a consonant are:
    a) First declension
    b) Second declension
    c) Third declension

3. Nouns that have stems ending in α or η are:
   a) First declension
   b) Second declension
   c) Third declension

4. The nominative case refers to:
   a) A noun which is the object of a verb
   b) A noun which is the subject of a verb
   c) A noun which expresses possession
   d) A noun which is an indirect object of the verb

5. The accusative case refers to:
   a) A noun which expresses possession
   b) A noun which is the subject of a verb
   c) A noun which is an indirect object of the verb
   d) A noun which is the object of a verb

6. Which of the following words is in the accusative case?
   a) λόγος
   b) λόγου
   c) λόγον
   d) λόγῳ

7. Which of the following words is in the nominative case?
   a) γραφαῖς
   b) γραφή
   c) γραφὴν
   d) γραφῶν

8. Which of the following words is in the nominative case?
   a) λόγον
   b) λόγοι
   c) λόγοις
   d) λόγους

9. When does οὐ become οὐκ?
   a) When it precedes a consonant
   b) When it precedes a verb

c) When it precedes a noun
d) When it precedes a vowel

10. Which of the following words is a definite article?
    a) ἐν
    b) δὲ
    c) ἆ
    d) ὁ

ANSWER KEY
1. B, 2. C, 3. A, 4. B, 5. D, 6. C, 7. B, 8. B, 9. D, 10. D

CHAPTER 7

Genitive and Dative

You Should Know

- What is the best translation for the word ἁμαρτία, -ας, ἡ?
  - Sin
- What is the best translation for the word ὥστε?
  - Therefore, so that
- What is the best translation for the word ἀρχή, -ῆς, ἡ?
  - Beginning
- What is the best translation for the word ἐξουσία, -ας, ἡ?
  - Authority, power
- What is the best translation for the word εὐαγγέλιον, -ου, τό?
  - Gospel
- What is the best translation for the word κύριος, -ου, ὁ?
  - Lord
- What is the best translation for the word υἱός, -οῦ, ὁ?
  - Son
- What is the best translation for the word οὐρανός, -οῦ, ὁ?
  - Heaven
- What is the best translation for the word γάρ?
  - For
- What is the best translation for the word μή?
  - Not
- The genitive case can indicate possession ("of"). The word it modifies is the head noun.

- The dative case can indicate the ideas of "to" (indirect object), "in," and "with."

- The indirect object indirectly receives the action of the verb. If you can put the word "to" in front of it, it is the indirect object. It answers the question "to whom?" or "to what?" It will be in the dative case, and you should use the key word "to" in your translation.

- Rule 4: In the dative singular, the ι subscripts if possible.

- Rule 5: Vowels often change their length ("ablaut").

- Rule 6: In the genitive and dative, the masculine and neuter will always be identical.

- If a first declension word has a stem ending in α where the preceding letter is ε, ι, or ρ, it will form the genitive and dative singular with α. Otherwise, the α will shift to η.

- When dividing a sentence into its parts, be sure to keep the article and the word in the genitive with the words they modify.

Quiz

1. The genitive case refers to:
    a) A noun which is the object of a verb
    b) A noun which is the subject of a verb
    c) A noun which expresses possession
    d) A noun which is an indirect object of the verb

2. The dative case refers to:
    a) A noun which expresses possession
    b) A noun which is the subject of a verb
    c) A noun which is an indirect object of the verb
    d) A noun which is the object of a verb

3. (T/F) Vowels do not change their length.

4. (T/F) In the dative singular, the ι subscripts if possible.

5. Which of the following words is in the genitive case?
   a) λόγος
   b) λόγου
   c) λόγον
   d) λόγῳ

6. Which of the following words is in the dative case?
   a) λόγος
   b) λόγου
   c) λόγον
   d) λόγῳ

7. Which of the following words is in the dative case?
   a) γραφαῖς
   b) γραφή
   c) γραφὴν
   d) γραφῶν

8. Which of the following words is in the genitive case?
   a) γραφῆς
   b) γραφῇ
   c) γραφὴν
   d) γραφῶν

9. What case is the definite article ὁ?
   a) Nominative
   b) Genitive
   c) Dative
   d) Accusative

10. What gender and case is the definite article ταῖς?
    a) Masculine nominative
    b) Feminine genitive
    c) Masculine dative
    d) Feminine dative

ANSWER KEY
1. C, 2. C, 3. F, 4. T, 5. B, 6. D, 7. A, 8. D, 9. A, 10. D

CHAPTER 8

Prepositions and εἰμί

You Should Know

- What is the best translation for the word παραβολή, -ῆς, ἡ?
  - Parable
- What is the best translation for the word ἀλλά?
  - But, yet, except
- What is the best translation for the word ὑπό (gen)?
  - By
- What is the best translation for the word ἀπό (gen)?
  - (Away) from
- What is the best translation for the word ὄχλος, -ου, ὁ?
  - Crowd, multitude
- What is the best translation for the word οἰκία, -ας, ἡ?
  - House
- What is the best translation for the word θάνατος, -ου, ὁ?
  - Death
- What is the best translation for the word θάλασσα, -ης, ἡ?
  - Sea, lake
- What is the best translation for the word διά (acc)?
  - On account of
- The word following the preposition is the object of the preposition, and the preposition and its object and modifiers form a prepositional phrase.

- The meaning of a preposition is determined by the case of its object. Always memorize the prepositions with the case(s) of their objects.
- Do not use the key words when translating the object of a preposition.
- Prepositions are not inflected, but their endings can change depending on the following word.
- A dependent clause cannot contain the main subject and verb in a sentence.
- The article is often omitted from Greek prepositional phrases. You can supply "the" if required by context.

Quiz

1. A preposition is:
    a) A word which is the object of a verb
    b) A word which describes the relationship between two words
    c) A word which expresses strong emotion
    d) A word which is only used with participles

2. The basic part of a verb is called the:
    a) Personal ending
    b) Stem
    c) Phrase
    d) Subject

3. What is the best translation for the word εἰμί?
    a) You are
    b) I am
    c) He, she, or it is
    d) They are

4. What is the best translation for the word ἐστίν?
    a) You are
    b) I am
    c) He, she, or it is
    d) They are

5. What is the nu at the end of ἐστίν called?
   a) Paragogic nun
   b) Movable Nu
   c) Silent Nu
   d) Liquid Nu

6. What is the past tense of ἐστίν?
   a) ἦσαν
   b) ἦν
   c) ἔστε
   d) ἔσομαι

7. The words ὅτι and ἵνα introduce what kind of clause?
   a) Independent clause
   b) Dependent clause
   c) Relative clause
   d) Participial clause

8. The word for "under" is:
   a) ἐξ
   b) πρός
   c) ὑπό + accusative
   d) ὑπό + dative

9. The word for "into" is:
   a) ἐξ
   b) μετά + acc
   c) ὑπό + accusative
   d) εἰς

10. The word for "to" is:
    a) μετά
    b) πρός
    c) ὑπό + accusative
    d) μετά + acc

ANSWER KEY
1. B, 2. B, 3. B, 4. C, 5. B, 6. B, 7. B, 8. C, 9. D, 10. B

CHAPTER 9

Adjectives

You Should Know

- What is the best translation for the word τρίτος, -η, -ον?
  - Third

- What is the best translation for the word αἰώνιος, -ον?
  - Eternal

- What is the best translation for the word πονηρός, -ά, -όν?
  - Evil

- What is the best translation for the word ἀλλήλων?
  - One another

- What is the best translation for the word ἐντολή, -ῆς, ἡ?
  - Commandment

- What is the best translation for the word νεκρός, -ά, -όν?
  - Dead

- What is the best translation for the word ἐάν?
  - If, when

- What is the best translation for the word κακός, -ή, -όν?
  - Bad, evil

- What is the best translation for the word δοῦλος, -ου, ὁ?
  - Slave, servant

- Adjectives can function as an attributive, a substantive, or a predicate.

- If the articular adjective modifies another word, then it is an attributive adjective. The attributive adjective agrees with the noun it modifies in case, number, and gender.

- If the articular adjective does not modify another word, then it is a substantival adjective. The case of the substantival adjective is determined by its function, its gender and number by what it stands for.

- If an anarthrous adjective occurs with an articular noun, the adjective is a predicate adjective and you may need to supply the verb "is."

- If there is no article before either the adjective or the other word, let context be your guide.

- A prepositional phrase preceded by the article can be an attributive modifier or a substantive.

- A 2-2 adjective has the same form in the masculine and feminine, and follows the second declension. The neuter likewise is second declension.

- A singular verb can be used when the subject is neuter plural and viewed as a whole.

Quiz

1. An adjective is:
   a) A word that is the object of a verb
   b) A word that describes a noun or a pronoun
   c) A word that describes a verb
   d) A word that is used for the subject of a sentence

2. An attributive adjective:
   a) Gives a quality of the word it is modifying
   b) Limits the range of meaning of the word it is modifying
   c) Functions as if it were a noun
   d) Gives a contrast to the word it is modifying

3. A substantive adjective:
   a) Functions as an implied verb in the sentence
   b) Gives a quality of the word it is modifying
   c) Functions as if it were a noun
   d) Gives the purpose of the verb in the sentence

4. A predicate adjective:
   a) Gives a quantity to the word it is modifying
   b) Asserts something about the subject, the "to be" verb is implied
   c) Functions as if it were a noun
   d) Gives the purpose of the verb in the sentence

5. What is the gender, case, and number of ἀγαθῆς?
   a) Feminine accusative, singular
   b) Masculine genitive, plural
   c) Feminine genitive, singular
   d) Neuter accusative, singular

6. What is the gender, case, and number of ἀγαθούς?
   a) Feminine accusative, plural
   b) Masculine accusative, plural
   c) Neuter genitive, plural
   d) Neuter accusative, singular

7. (T/F) If a definite article is followed by a prepositional phrase, it is generally best to translate the phrase as a relative clause (who, which).

8. The word for "son" is:
   a) υἱός
   b) ἦν
   c) φωνή
   d) ἵνα

9. The word for "as" is:
   a) υἱός
   b) καθώς

c) φωνή
d) ἦν

10. The word for "in order that" is:
   a) υἱός
   b) ἦν
   c) φωνή
   d) ἵνα

ANSWER KEY
1. B, 2. A, 3. C, 4. B, 5. C, 6. B, 7. T, 8. A, 9. B, 10. D

CHAPTER 10

Third Declension

You Should Know

- What is the best translation for the word τις, τι?
  – Someone, anyone
- What is the best translation for the word τέκνον, -ου, τό?
  – Child, descendant
- What is the best translation for the word τίς, τί?
  – Who? What? Which?
- What is the best translation for the word ἅγιος, -α, -ον?
  – Holy
- What is the best translation for the word σῶμα, -τος, τό?
  – Body
- What is the best translation for the word οὐδείς, οὐδεμία, οὐδέν?
  – No one, nothing
- What is the best translation for the word σάρξ, σαρκός, ἡ?
  – Flesh, body
- What is the best translation for the word πᾶς, πᾶσα, πᾶν?
  – Each, every, all
- What is the best translation for the word σύν (dat)?
  – With
- Words whose stems end in a consonant use third declension case endings.

- Memorize the genitive singular form with the lexical form; drop the case ending from the genitive singular to find the stem.

- Whatever happens in the nominative singular (ς) also happens in the dative plural (σι).

- ν and τ drop out before a σ, and τ at the end of a word.

- To remember the gender of a third declension noun, memorize its lexical form with the article. To remember the stem of a third declension noun, memorize its genitive form as well as the stem itself.

- Memorize the *Master Case Ending Chart* perfectly.

- Rule 7: The Square of Stops (including what happens when σ is added).

- Rule 8: A τ cannot stand at the end of a word and will drop off.

- ὁ δέ can be translated "but he," and the article before a prepositional phrase is probably signaling that the prepositional phrase is an attributive construction.

- πᾶς is a paradigmatic word for grammar yet to come (participles), so learn it well.

Quiz

1. The stem of a third declension noun:
    a) Ends in an omicron
    b) Ends in a consonant
    c) Ends in an alpha or eta
    d) Ends in an iota

2. An attributive adjective:
    a) Gives a quality of the word it is modifying
    b) Limits the range of meaning of the word it is modifying
    c) Functions as if it were a noun
    d) Gives a contrast to the word it is modifying

3. When a sigma is added to stem ending in nu:
   a) The nu doubles
   b) The nu drops out
   c) The nu and sigma combine
   d) The sigma drops out

4. What is the case and number of σαρκός?
   a) Accusative, singular
   b) Genitive, plural
   c) Genitive, singular
   d) Dative, singular

5. What is the case and number of σαρκί?
   a) Genitive, plural
   b) Nominative, singular
   c) Genitive, singular
   d) Dative, singular

6. What is the case and number of ὀνόματα?
   a) Nominative, plural
   b) Genitive, singular
   c) Accusative, singular
   d) Dative, plural

7. According to the "square of stops," what do the letters β and σ combine to form?
   a) ψ
   b) χ
   c) ξ
   d) θ

8. According to the "square of stops," what do the letters κ and σ combine to form?
   a) ψ
   b) χ
   c) ξ
   d) θ

9. (T/F) The *dental* consonants are τ and δ.
10. (T/F) The *velar* consonants are π and σ.

ANSWER KEY

1. B, 2. A, 3. B, 4. C, 5. D, 6. A, 7. A, 8. C, 9. T, 10. F

CHAPTER 11

First and Second Person; Personal Pronouns

You Should Know

- What is the best translation for the word ὧδε?
  - Here, hither

- What is the best translation for the word ἀδελφός, -οῦ, ὁ?
  - Brother

- What is the best translation for the word μήτηρ, -τρός, ἡ?
  - Mother

- What is the best translation for the word πατήρ, πατρός, ὁ?
  - Father

- What is the best translation for the word θέλημα, -τος, τό?
  - Will

- What is the best translation for the word ἐκκλησία, -ας, ἡ?
  - Church

- What is the best translation for the word ὕδωρ, ὕδατος, τό?
  - Water

- What is the best translation for the word πίστις, -εως, ἡ?
  - Faith, belief

- What is the best translation for the word φῶς, -φωτός, τό?
  - Light

- A personal pronoun is a word replacing a personal noun that is its antecedent.

- The case of a pronoun is determined by its function in the sentence, number and person by its antecedent.

- Pronouns are first person (the person speaking), second person (the person spoken to), or third person (that which is spoken about).

- The English personal pronouns are "I, my, me, we, our, us" (first person) and "you, your" (second person).

- First and second person pronouns agree with their antecedent in person and number. Their case is determined by their function in the sentence.

- Personal pronouns in oblique cases can have accents when they are used emphatically. The first person singular pronoun can also have an initial ε.

- πίστις-type words end in a consonantal iota, which now appears as ι or ε, and are all feminine.

Quiz

1. A pronoun is:
    a) A word that replaces another noun
    b) A word that describes another noun
    c) A noun that must stand first in the sentence
    d) A noun that is only used with prepositions

2. The number of a pronoun is determined by:
    a) Its function in the sentence
    b) The nominative case
    c) The accusative case
    d) The antecedent

3. The first person singular personal pronoun in English is:
    a) He
    b) She
    c) I
    d) They

4. The third person plural personal pronoun in English is:
   a) You
   b) I
   c) We
   d) They

5. Which *person* is the Greek pronoun σύ?
   a) First
   b) Second
   c) Third

6. Which *person* is the Greek pronoun ἐγώ?
   a) First
   b) Second
   c) Third

7. Which *case, number, and person* is the Greek pronoun ἡμᾶς?
   a) Nominative singular, first person
   b) Nominative plural, second person
   c) Accusative singular, first person
   d) Accusative plural, first person

8. Which *case, number, and person* is the Greek pronoun ὑμεῖς?
   a) Nominative singular, second person
   b) Nominative plural, second person
   c) Genitive singular, first person
   d) Dative plural, first person

9. (T/F) In Greek, the case of a pronoun is determined by its function in the sentence.

10. What is the lexical form of ὑμεῖς?
    a) σε
    b) σύ
    c) ἡμεῖς
    d) ἐγώ

ANSWER KEY

1. A, 2. D, 3. C, 4. D, 5. B, 6. A, 7. D, 8. B, 9. T, 10. B

CHAPTER 12

αὐτός

You Should Know

- What is the best translation for the word διδάσκαλος, -ου, ὁ?
  – Teacher
- What is the best translation for the word ὀφθαλμός, -οῦ, ὁ?
  – Eye
- What is the best translation for the word μαθητής, -οῦ, ὁ?
  – Disciple
- What is the best translation for the word πούς, ποδός, ὁ?
  – Foot
- What is the best translation for the word εὐθύς?
  – Immediately
- What is the best translation for the word πάλιν?
  – Again
- What is the best translation for the word ὅπως?
  – How, that, in order that
- What is the best translation for the word ὑπέρ (gen)?
  – In behalf of
- What is the best translation for the word ἕως?
  – Until, as far as
- What is the best translation for the word αἰών, -ῶνος, ὁ?
  – Age, eternity

- Pronouns have many different uses in Greek. One of the most common pronouns is αὐτός. Its ordinary use is to "stand in" for a noun to avoid repetition.

- αὐτός uses the normal case endings except for the nominative and accusative neuter singular, which drop the ν.

- When αὐτός functions as a pronoun, its case is determined by function, its number and gender by antecedent.

- When αὐτός adds emphasis, it can be translated with the reflexive pronoun. It usually will be in the predicate position, in the nominative case.

- αὐτός can function as the identical adjective and is translated "same." In this usage it normally is in the attributive position.

Quiz

1. Which of the following is/are a use of αὐτός?
    a) Personal pronoun
    b) Adjectival intensive
    c) Identical adjective
    d) All of the above
    e) A & B
    f) A & C

2. The third person plural personal pronoun in English is:
    a) It
    b) She
    c) I
    d) They

3. Which *case, number, and gender* is the following Greek pronoun: αὐταῖς?
    a) Nominative plural, masculine
    b) Dative plural, feminine
    c) Nominative singular, masculine
    d) Accusative plural, feminine

4. Which *case, number, and gender* is the following Greek pronoun: αὐτήν?

   a) Accusative plural, masculine
   b) Dative plural, neuter
   c) Genitive singular, masculine
   d) Accusative singular, feminine

5. Which *case, number, and gender* is the following Greek pronoun: αὐτό?

   a) Nominative singular, neuter
   b) Genitive plural, feminine
   c) Dative singular, neuter
   d) Accusative plural, feminine

6. Which *case, number, and gender* is the following Greek pronoun: αὐτοί?

   a) Nominative plural, neuter
   b) Genitive plural, neuter
   c) Nominative plural, masculine
   d) Dative plural, feminine

7. The pronoun αὐτός may be used as an adjective in the predicate position, which functions to:

   a) Clarify the word it modifies
   b) Intensify the word it modifies
   c) Negate the word it modifies
   d) Expand on the word it modifies

8. The pronoun αὐτός may be used as an identical adjective, which is often translated:

   a) "The same"
   b) "Himself"
   c) "They"
   d) "Since" or "Because"

9. The word for "therefore" is:

   a) οὖν
   b) ἀλλά

c) μηδείς
   d) μόνος

10. The word for "but" is:
    a) οὖν
    b) ἀλλά
    c) μηδείς
    d) μόνος

ANSWER KEY
1. D, 2. D, 3. B, 4. D, 5. A, 6. C, 7. B, 8. A, 9. A, 10. B

CHAPTER 13

Demonstrative Pronouns and Adjectives
οὗτος, ἐκεῖνος

You Should Know

- What is the best translation for the word σημεῖον, -ου, τό?
  - Sign, miracle
- What is the best translation for the word δικαιοσύνη, -ης, ἡ?
  - Righteousness
- What is the best translation for the word μέγας, μεγάλη, μέγα?
  - Large, great
- What is the best translation for the word δώδεκα?
  - Twelve
- What is the best translation for the word πόλις, -εως, ἡ?
  - City
- What is the best translation for the word ἑαυτοῦ, -ῆς, -οῦ?
  - Himself, herself, itself
- What is the best translation for the word πῶς?
  - How?
- What is the best translation for the word γυνή, -αικός, ἡ?
  - Woman
- The demonstrative "this/these" is οὗτος and "that/those" is ἐκεῖνος. οὗτος always begins with either a rough breathing or τ.

Neither uses a case ending in the nominative/accusative neuter singular, and the final stem vowel has shifted to υ.

- When the demonstratives function as a pronoun, their case is determined by their function in the sentence, number and gender by their antecedent. You can supply a helping word if you wish, determined by natural gender.

- When they function as an adjective, their case, number, and gender agree with the word they are modifying. They will always be in the predicate position although they are translated as attributive adjectives.

- A demonstrative can weaken in force and be used as a personal pronoun.

- The vocative is the case of direct address.

- In the plural, it is identical to the nominative regardless of declension.

- In the singular first declension, it is identical to the nominative.

- In the singular second declension, it usually has the case ending ε.

- In the singular third declension, it usually is the bare stem.

Quiz

1. A demonstrative pronoun is translated:
    a) Since
    b) This / these
    c) He, she, it
    d) Which

2. Which *case, number, and gender* is the Greek demonstrative pronoun ταῦτα?
    a) Accusative plural, masculine
    b) Nominative plural, neuter
    c) Genitive singular, neuter
    d) Dative plural, feminine

3. Which *case, number, and gender* is the Greek pronoun τούτου?

   a) Accusative plural, feminine
   b) Dative singular, neuter
   c) Genitive singular, masculine
   d) Genitive singular, feminine

4. Which *case, number, and gender* is the Greek pronoun τούτῳ?

   a) Genitive plural, neuter
   b) Dative plural, feminine
   c) Dative singular, neuter
   d) Accusative plural, masculine

5. Which *case, number, and gender* is the Greek pronoun ἐκείνης?

   a) Nominative singular, neuter
   b) Genitive singular, feminine
   c) Dative plural, masculine
   d) Accusative plural, feminine

6. Which *case, number, and gender* is the Greek pronoun ἐκείνους?

   a) Nominative plural, neuter
   b) Genitive singular, feminine
   c) Dative singular, masculine
   d) Accusative plural, masculine

7. How does the vocative case function?

   a) Instrument of the verb
   b) Result of the verb
   c) Direct address
   d) It appears only in the predicate

8. Which of the following nouns is in the vocative case?

   a) κύριος
   b) κυρίου
   c) κύριε
   d) κύριον

9. Which of the following English words is the comparative degree of the adjective?

a) Large
b) Larger
c) Largest
d) None of the above

10. What is it called when one word is formed by combining two (such as κἀγώ)?
    a) Ellipsis
    b) Crasis
    c) Elision
    d) Diaresis

ANSWER KEY
1. B, 2. B, 3. C, 4. C, 5. B, 6. D, 7. C, 8. C, 9. B, 10. B

CHAPTER 14

Relative Pronoun

You Should Know

- What is the best translation for the word ψυχή, -ῆς, ἡ?
  – Soul, life
- What is the best translation for the word εἰρήνη, -ης, ἡ?
  – Peace
- What is the best translation for the word χείρ, χειρός, ἡ?
  – Hand
- What is the best translation for the word ἐπαγγελία, -ας, ἡ?
  – Promise
- What is the best translation for the word κεφαλή, -ῆς, ἡ?
  – Head
- What is the best translation for the word θρόνος, -ου, ὁ?
  – Throne
- What is the best translation for the word ὁδός, -οῦ, ἡ?
  – Way, road, journey
- What is the best translation for the word ἑπτά?
  – Seven
- What is the best translation for the word πλοῖον, -ου, τό?
  – Boat, ship
- What is the best translation for the word ἀλήθεια, -ας, ἡ?
  – Truth

- Relative pronouns introduce relative clauses, which are capable of performing many of the tasks of nouns and adjectives.

- The relative pronouns are ὅς, ἥ, and ὅ. They follow the normal 2-1-2 declension patterns (like αὐτός) and always have a rough breathing and an accent.

- The case of a relative pronoun is determined by its use in the relative clause, and its number and gender by its antecedent.

- You can add a word to your translation of a relative clause; use your educated common sense and context to determine the best pronoun.

- Relative clauses are always dependent.

Quiz

1. A relative pronoun is translated:
    a) Who / which / that
    b) This / these
    c) That / those
    d) He, she, or it

2. In Matthew 1:16 "... and Jacob the father of Joseph, the husband of Mary, *of whom* was born Jesus, who is called Christ," NIV 1984), to whom do the words "*of whom*" refer to, based on the Greek pronoun used?
    a) Joseph as father
    b) Mary as mother
    c) Both Joseph and Mary as parents
    d) God as Father

3. Which *case, number, and gender* is the Greek relative pronoun οἷς?
    a) Accusative plural, feminine
    b) Accusative plural, neuter
    c) Genitive singular, feminine
    d) Dative plural, masculine

4. Which *case, number, and gender* is the Greek pronoun αἵ?

   a) Nominative plural, feminine
   b) Dative singular, neuter
   c) Dative singular, masculine
   d) Nominative singular, feminine

5. Which *case, number, and gender* is the Greek pronoun ἧς?

   a) Genitive singular, neuter
   b) Nominative plural, feminine
   c) Genitive singular, feminine
   d) Accusative plural, neuter

6. Which *case, number, and gender* is the Greek pronoun ᾧ?

   a) Accusative plural, feminine
   b) Genitive singular, feminine
   c) Dative singular, masculine
   d) Accusative plural, neuter

7. Which *case, number, and gender* is the Greek pronoun ὅ?

   a) Accusative singular, neuter
   b) Genitive singular, neuter
   c) Dative plural, masculine
   d) Accusative plural, feminine

8. When phrasing, it is a good idea to connect the relative cause to the antecedent by:

   a) Placing the relative pronoun under the antecedent
   b) Dividing up the sentence by relative causes
   c) By ignoring it altogether for translating purposes
   d) Using a system of lines and dashes to connect antecedents and relative pronouns

9. The word for "when" is:

   a) ὅτε
   b) κἀγώ
   c) κατά
   d) ῥῆμα

10. The word for "and I" is:
    a) ὅτε
    b) κἀγώ
    c) κατά
    d) ῥῆμα

ANSWER KEY
1. A, 2. B, 3. D, 4. A, 5. C, 6. C, 7. A, 8. A, 9. A, 10. B

CHAPTER 15

Introduction to Verbs

You Should Know

- What is the best translation for the word λέγω?
  - I say

- A verb agrees with its subject in person (first; second; third) and number (singular; plural).

- Agreement is accomplished through the use of personal endings.

- The true significance of the Greek verb is its ability to describe aspect. A verb can be imperfective, which means the process it describes is a continuous action. Or a Greek verb can be perfective, which means that the author is not giving us a clue as to the true nature of the action other than to say that it occurred.

- "Tense" describes the form of the verb. "Time" describes when the action of the verb occurs.

- Voice can be active (i.e., the subject does the action), passive (i.e., the subject receives the action of the verb), or middle (which we are equating with the active for the time being).

- The indicative mood is the dominant mood, used to make a statement of fact or ask a question.

- The root is the basic form of a word; the stem of a verb is the form of the root in a particular tense. A verb is composed of a tense stem, connecting vowel, and personal ending.

- Parsing a verb means to identify its person, number, tense, voice, mood, lexical form, and definition of the inflected form.

- The lexical form of a verb is the first person singular, present indicative.
- A morpheme is the smallest unit of meaning.

Quiz

1. The "aspect" of a verb refers to:
    a) The time of the action
    b) The kind of the action
    c) A conditional verb
    d) A subjective action

2. The phrase "I studied last night" is an example of what kind of verbal aspect?
    a) Completed
    b) Conditional
    c) Continuous
    d) Contemporary

3. Another way to describe a "completed action" is:
    a) Continuous
    b) Punctiliar
    c) Reserved
    d) Functional

4. The aspect of a verb refers to:
    a) The relationship between a verb and reality
    b) The relationship between the subject and the verb
    c) Both the time when the action of the verb takes place and the form of the verb
    d) The kind of action

5. The voice of a verb refers to:
    a) The relationship between the subject and object
    b) The relationship of the verb and a prepositional phrase
    c) The relationship between the subject and verb
    d) The kind of action

6. The mood of a verb refers to:
   a) The relationship between a verb and reality
   b) Both the time when the action of the verb takes place and the form of the verb
   c) The relationship between verb and a subject
   d) The kind of action

7. Which of the following phrases is in the passive voice?
   a) He hit the ball
   b) She studied Greek
   c) Bill was hit by the ball
   d) The cat slept all day

8. What are personal endings in Greek?
   a) Suffixes added after the connecting vowel so the verb agrees with its subject
   b) Personal pronouns added to a relative clause so the verb agrees with its subject
   c) Relative clauses that indicate person and number
   d) Connecting vowels to help with pronunciation

9. The lexical form of a verb is always:
   a) First person singular, present indicative
   b) First person plural, present subjunctive
   c) First person singular, future indicative
   d) Third person plural, future subjunctive

10. A morpheme is:
    a) The smallest unit of meaning
    b) A personal ending
    c) A connecting vowel
    d) A & B
    e) B & C

ANSWER KEY

1. B, 2. A, 3. B, 4. D, 5. C, 6. A, 7. C, 8. A, 9. A, 10. D

CHAPTER 16

Present Active Indicative

You Should Know

- What is the best translation for the word χαρά, -ᾶς, ἡ?
  – Joy
- What is the best translation for the word βλέπω?
  – I see
- What is the best translation for the word λύω?
  – I loose, untie, destroy
- What is the best translation for the word πιστεύω?
  – I believe
- What is the best translation for the word ἔχω?
  – I have
- What is the best translation for the word νόμος, -ου, ὁ?
  – Law
- What is the best translation for the word τότε?
  – Then
- What is the best translation for the word ὅπου?
  – Where, whither
- What is the best translation for the word τυφλός, -ή, -όν?
  – Blind
- The present active indicative describes an action that usually occurs in the present time.

- The present tense verb is composed of three parts: present verbal stem, connecting vowel, and primary personal ending.
- The root is the most basic form of a verb; its stem is the form of the root in a particular tense.
- In the indicative mood, if the personal ending begins with μ or ν, the connecting vowel is ο; otherwise the connecting vowel is ε. If there is no personal ending, the connecting vowel can be either ο or ε.
- A verb agrees with its subject in person and number.
- The present active tense uses the primary active endings: ω, εις, ει, ομεν, ετε, ουσι(ν). The real personal endings are—ς, ι, μεν, τε, νσι.
- A movable nu can be added to the third person plural personal ending.
- Personal pronouns in the nominative are generally emphasizing the subject, often in contrast to someone else.

Quiz

1. The present active indicative verb is formed by:
   a) Present stem + connecting vowel + case endings
   b) Present stem + connecting vowel + personal endings
   c) Present stem + personal endings
   d) Present stem + connecting vowel + secondary endings

2. What is the *person and number* of the verb λέγει?
   a) First singular
   b) Second plural
   c) Third singular
   d) Second singular

3. What is the *person and number* of the verb λέγετε?
   a) Third singular
   b) Second plural

c) First plural
d) Second singular

4. What is the *person and number* of the verb λέγουσιν?

    a) First plural
    b) Second plural
    c) Third plural
    d) Second singular

5. What is the *person and number* of the verb λέγομεν?

    a) First plural
    b) Second singular
    c) Third plural
    d) First singular

6. What is the *person and number* of the verb λέγω?

    a) Second plural
    b) Third singular
    c) First singular
    d) Second singular

7. What is the best translation of the verb λέγεις?

    a) He says
    b) They said
    c) You are saying
    d) We are saying

8. What is the explanation for the nu at the end of λέγουσιν?

    a) It confirms that the verb is present active indicative
    b) It is a movable nu
    c) It indicates the verb has a continuous aspect
    d) It is usually added to the primary endings

9. The present active tense uses which of the following primary active endings?

    a) ω
    b) εις

c) ει
d) ομεν
e) ετε
f) All of the above
g) A & B

10. The verb ἀγαπᾷ in 2 Corinthians 9:7, "God loves a cheerful giver," is used to emphasize:
   a) Continuous action
   b) A timeless fact
   c) An action occurring at the same time
   d) An action that happens immediately

ANSWER KEY
1. B, 2. C, 3. B, 4. C, 5. A, 6. C, 7. C, 8. B, 9. F, 10. B

CHAPTER 17

Contract Verbs

You Should Know

- What is the best translation for the word τηρέω?
  - I keep, guard, observe
- What is the best translation for the word ἀγαπάω?
  - I love, cherish
- What is the best translation for the word ποιέω?
  - I do, make
- What is the best translation for the word λαλέω?
  - I speak, say
- What is the best translation for the word πληρόω?
  - I fill, fulfill
- What is the best translation for the word δαιμόνιον, -ου, τό?
  - Demon
- What is the best translation for the word ζητέω?
  - I seek, desire
- What is the best translation for the word καλέω?
  - I call, name, invite
- Contract verbs have roots ending in α, ε, or ο.
- The Big Five: ου is formed from εο, οε, and οο; ει is formed from εε; ω is formed from almost any combination of ο or ω with any other vowel, except for rule 1; α is formed from αε; η is formed from εα.
- οι is formed from οει.

- If the contract vowel and the first vowel of the diphthong are the *same*, they simplify.

- If the contract vowel and the first vowel of the diphthong are *different*, they contract. If the second vowel of the diphthong is ι, it subscripts if possible; if it is υ and the final letter of the newly contracted diphthong is υ, they simplify to a single υ.

- Contract verbs contract as if the personal endings are those visible in the present active indicative.

- In the first person singular, no personal ending is used so the connecting vowel ο lengthens to ω.

- The lexical form shows the contract vowel (ἀγαπάω), but if that form actually occurs in the text, the contract vowel and ο will have contracted (ἀγαπῶ, ποιῶ, πληρῶ).

- Transitive verbs require an object, intransitive verbs do not.

Quiz

1. A contract verb is:
   a) A verb with a stem ending in mu or nu
   b) A verb with a stem which reduces syllables when endings are added
   c) A verb stem ending with alpha, epsilon or omicron
   d) A verb which ends in a double-sigma

2. The contraction ου is formed by the following combinations:
   a) εο, οε, οο
   b) αο, αι
   c) ει, εε
   d) εει

3. The contraction ει is formed by the following combinations:
   a) εο, οε, οο
   b) αο, αι

c) ει, εε
d) εει

4. (T/F) Almost any combination of omicron and omega will contract to omega, except εο, οε, οο.

5. The contraction η is formed by the following combinations:
   a) εο, οε, οο
   b) εα
   c) ει, εε
   d) ηυ

6. What is the *person and number* of the verb ἀγαπᾷς?
   a) First singular
   b) Second plural
   c) Third singular
   d) Second singular

7. What is the *person and number* of the verb πληροῖς?
   a) Third singular
   b) Second plural
   c) First plural
   d) Second singular

8. A transitive verb:
   a) Carries the force of its action over to an object
   b) Requires no direct object
   c) Shows the presence of modifiers
   d) All of the above

9. The digamma:
   a) Is pronounced "fh"
   b) Is still a letter in the Greek alphabet
   c) Explains some apparent irregularities in the Greek language
   d) Is known as the "triple gamma"

10. The translation of this word can sometimes be quite idiomatic and has a wide range of meaning:

a) τηρέω
b) ποιέω
c) ζητέω
d) ἀγαπάω

ANSWER KEY
1. C, 2. A, 3. C, 4. T, 5. B, 6. D, 7. B, 8. A, 9. C, 10. B

CHAPTER 18

Present Middle/ Passive Indicative

You Should Know

- What is the best translation for the word τόπος, -ου, ὁ?
  - Place, location
- What is the best translation for the word ἀποκρίνομαι?
  - I answer
- What is the best translation for the word συνάγω?
  - I gather together
- What is the best translation for the word δεῖ?
  - It is necessary
- What is the best translation for the word πορεύομαι?
  - I come, proceed, live
- What is the best translation for the word νύξ, νυκτός, ἡ?
  - Night
- What is the best translation for the word δύναμαι?
  - I am able, am powerful
- What is the best translation for the word ὅστις, ἥτις, ὅτι?
  - Whoever, whichever, whatever
- What is the best translation for the word ἔρχομαι?
  - I come, go

- What is the best translation for the word ὡς?
  - As, like, when, that
- If a verb is in the passive voice, the subject is receiving the action of the verb.
- To form the English passive you add a helping verb. The time of an English verb that has helping verbs is determined by the time of the helping verb.
- The present middle/passive in Greek is formed by joining the present tense stem with the connecting vowel and the primary middle/passive endings. The primary middle/passive personal endings are μαι, σαι (which changes to η when joined with the connecting vowel), ται, μεθα, σθε, νται.
- Verbs in the middle describe an action that in some way affects the subject ("subject-affectedness"), and you will translate these verbs as actives.
- Verbs that occur in the middle but not in the active in our literature generally have lexical forms ending in ομαι and are called "middle-only" or "deponent."
- Look for contextual clues to determine if a verb is middle or passive: lexical forms ending in ομαι are probably middle; verbs followed by something indicating agency are probably passive; verbs indicating change or personal grooming are probably middle; if active does not make sense, try passive.

Quiz

1. In the passive voice:
    a) The subject is the one performing the action
    b) The subject is omitted from the sentence
    c) The subject is the one receiving the action
    d) The subject is implied by the context

2. What is subject-affectedness?
    a) The subject is affected by the action of the verb
    b) The verb is affected by the person and number of the subject
    c) The middle voice is reflexive or reciprocal
    d) The direct object only receives the action of the verb

3. Matthew 7:7, "Ask and it will be given to you," is an example of which of the following?
    a) Slight subject affectedness
    b) A middle-only verb
    c) Lack of a connecting vowel
    d) A & C
    e) None of the above

4. Which of the following tend to be middle verbs?
    a) Verbs that describe different facets of grooming
    b) Verbs that describe change
    c) Verbs that describe spontaneous processes
    d) Verbs that involve two participants
    e) Verbs that describe emotion
    f) All of the above

5. What is the *person and number* of the verb λύομαι?
    a) First singular
    b) Second plural
    c) Third singular
    d) Second singular

6. What is the *person and number* of the verb λύεσθε?
    a) Third singular
    b) Second plural
    c) Third plural
    d) Second singular

7. What is the *person and number* of the verb λύῃ?
    a) Third singular
    b) Third plural
    c) First singular
    d) Second singular

8. A deponent verb is:
    a) An active verb with a middle/passive meaning
    b) A verb with no active form; the middle/passive serves as the active
    c) A verb always translated as a passive regardless of form
    d) A verb which never appears in the passive
    e) None of the above

9. (T/F) The only way to tell if a verb is deponent is by its lexical form.

10. (T/F) The forms of the middle are quite different than the passive.

ANSWER KEY
1. C, 2. A, 3. A, 4. F, 5. A, 6. B, 7. D, 8. B, 9. T, 10. F

CHAPTER 19

Future Active and Middle Indicative

You Should Know

- What is the best translation for the word προσκυνέω?
  - I worship
- What is the best translation for the word γεννάω?
  - I beget, give birth
- What is the best translation for the word ζάω?
  - I live
- What is the best translation for the word βασιλεύς, -έως, ὁ?
  - King
- What is the best translation for the word καρπός, -οῦ, ὁ?
  - Fruit
- What is the best translation for the word ὅλος, -η, -ον?
  - Whole
- The future tense indicates an action that will occur in the future. It is translated with the undefined form of the verb.
- The roots of pattern 1 verbs are used without modification in the formation of the present and future tense stems (roots ending in ι or υ, contract verbs, and roots ending in a stop). The present and future tense stems are therefore identical.
- The future active can be formed from the future tense stem + tense formative (σ) + connecting vowel + primary active personal endings.

- Contract verbs lengthen their contract vowel before a tense formative.

- Knowing the Square of Stops is especially useful in the future tense. When joined with a σ, labials go to ψ, velars go to ξ, and dentals drop out.

- You should memorize the future of εἰμί.

Quiz

1. What is the tense sign for the future?
    a) A sigma prefixed to the root
    b) A sigma between the future active stem and the primary endings
    c) A sigma added to the end of the primary endings
    d) The helping verb "will"

2. Which of the following is NOT a category of pattern 1 verbal roots?
    a) Roots ending in ι or υ
    b) Contract verbs
    c) Roots ending in a stop
    d) Words using different roots

3. In the Old Testament, the future tense is often used to:
    a) Give a simple prediction
    b) Denote casual speech
    c) Indicate an action occurring in the future
    d) Give a command

4. What are the *person and number* of the verb λύσει?
    a) First singular
    b) Second plural
    c) Second singular
    d) Third singular

5. What are the *person and number* of the verb λύσουσι?

a) First singular
b) Second plural
c) Third plural
d) Second singular

6. What are the *person and number* of the verb λυσόμεθα?

    a) Third singular
    b) First plural
    c) Third plural
    d) Second singular

7. A sigma and a labial consonant (π, β, φ) will combine to form:

    a) η
    b) ψ
    c) ξ
    d) χ

8. A sigma and a velar consonant (κ, γ, χ) will combine to form:

    a) ψ
    b) σ
    c) ξ
    d) The consonant drops out

9. The word for "I hear" is:

    a) μείζων
    b) ἀκούω
    c) θέλημα
    d) χάρις

10. The word for "I remain" is:

    a) πορεύομαι
    b) μένω
    c) μείζων
    d) πίστις

ANSWER KEY

1. B, 2. D, 3. D, 4. D, 5. C, 6. B, 7. B, 8. C, 9. B, 10. B

CHAPTER 20

Verbal Roots (Patterns 2–4)

You Should Know

- What is the best translation for the word σῴζω?
  - I save
- What is the best translation for the word αἴρω?
  - I raise, take up
- What is the best translation for the word ὁράω?
  - I see, notice
- What is the best translation for the word ἀποκτείνω?
  - I kill
- What is the best translation for the word μένω?
  - I remain
- What is the best translation for the word ἀποστέλλω?
  - I send (away)
- What is the best translation for the word ἐκβάλλω?
  - I cast out
- What is the best translation for the word ἐγείρω?
  - I raise up
- What is the best translation for the word γινώσκω?
  - I know

- What is the best translation for the word στόμα, -τος, τό?
  - Mouth
- The root of a verb is its most basic form. The stem of a verb is the basic form of that verb in a particular tense.
- All tense stems are formed from the verbal root; the present tense stem is not the basis for the other tenses.
- There are four patterns of how the verbal root forms the present tense stem.
- Pattern 1: Verbal root and present tense stem are the same. This includes roots ending in ι or υ, contract verbs, and roots ending in a stop.
- Pattern 2: The verb uses different roots.
- Pattern 3: Liquid roots (λ, μ, ν, ρ) are generally used without modification (except for ablaut) in the present and future active stems. They use εσ as the tense formative in the future. The σ drops out and the ε contracts with the connecting vowel. They look just like present tense epsilon contract verbs.
- Pattern 4: The verbal root is regularly modified to form the present tense stem. This includes verbal roots ending in a stop (ιζω, αζω, σσω), stems ending in a double consonant, and roots that add one or more letter(s) (ισκ). The root will usually be clearly visible in the other tense stems.
- A compound verb follows the tense forms of the simple verb.

Quiz

1. What is a liquid verb?
    a) A verb which has a unique aorist form
    b) A verb whose stem ends in a liquid consonant
    c) A verb which regularly omits consonants in its present stem
    d) A verb which ends in a double sigma

2. What are the liquid consonants?
    a) π, β, φ
    b) τ, δ, θ
    c) λ, μ, ν, ρ
    d) κ, γ, χ

3. How do you explain the variation between ἔρχομαι (present) and ἐλεύσομαι (future)?
    a) The present and future are formed from different roots
    b) The present and future are formed from different stems
    c) The present and future have different personal endings
    d) The present and future have different connecting vowels

4. What is the "consonantal iota"?
    a) Verbs whose present tense stems end in ιζω or αζω
    b) Verbs that have vowels changing their length or dropping out
    c) A letter in the Greek alphabet which causes difficult changes in tense stems
    d) A root that adds σκ or ισκ to form the present tense stem

5. (T/F) Liquid future verbs have a different meaning than the non-liquid futures.

6. (T/F) Accents can be helpful for identifying liquid verbs since they always have a circumflex accent over contracted vowels.

7. (T/F) Some verb roots add an iota in the present tense.

8. (T/F) Compound verbs form their tense stems the same way as the simple verb.

9. Roots with double consonants in the present tense regularly modify by:
    a) Dropping both of the consonants
    b) Dropping one of the double consonants
    c) Replacing the second consonant with a sigma
    d) Replacing the first consonant with an epsilon
    e) A & C
    f) None of the above

10. A compound verb:
   a) Combines two or more verbs
   b) Combines a noun and a verb
   c) Combines a preposition and a verb
   d) Combines a liquid and non-liquid verb

ANSWER KEY
1. B, 2. C, 3. A, 4. C, 5. F, 6. T, 7. T, 8. T, 9. B, 10. C

CHAPTER 21

Imperfect Indicative

You Should Know

- What is the best translation for the word χρόνος, -ου, ὁ?
  - Time

- What is the best translation for the word ἀκολουθέω?
  - I follow

- What is the best translation for the word περιπατέω?
  - I walk (around), live

- What is the best translation for the word ἐπερωτάω?
  - I ask (for), a question

- What is the best translation for the word θέλω?
  - I will, wish, desire

- What is the best translation for the word συναγωγή, -ῆς, ἡ?
  - Synagogue, meeting

- The imperfect tense indicates an imperfective action usually in the past.

- The imperfect is formed with an augment + present tense stem + connecting vowel + secondary endings. The imperfect is a secondary tense because it employs an augment.

- The augment is a prefix attached to the verb indicating past time.

- If the stem begins with a consonant, the augment is ε.

- If the stem begins with a single vowel, the vowel lengthens.

- If the stem begins with a diphthong, either the first vowel of the diphthong lengthens or the diphthong is not changed.
- If it is a compound verb, the verbal part is augmented. If the preposition ends in a vowel it will either drop off or not contract with the augment.
- The secondary personal endings are similar to the primary—active: ν, ς, μεν, τε, ν; passive: μην, σο, το, μεθα, σθε, ντο.
- A verb that is middle only (deponent) in the present will also be middle only in the imperfect.
- Contract verbs follow the regular rules.

Quiz

1. These tenses have augments in the indicative to indicate past tense:
   a) Perfect and imperfect
   b) Perfect and aorist
   c) Imperfect and aorist
   d) Perfect and pluperfect

2. An imperfect verb describes:
   a) A complete action which is usually in the past
   b) An incomplete action which is usually in the past
   c) An incomplete action which is usually in the present
   d) A complete action which is usually in the present

3. An aorist verb describes:
   a) A complete action which is usually in the past
   b) An incomplete action which is usually in the past
   c) An incomplete action which is usually in the present
   d) A complete action which is usually in the present

4. What is an augment?
   a) An epsilon prefixed to a verb
   b) An epsilon suffixed to a verb
   c) An alpha prefixed to a verb
   d) An epsilon added to the root before the personal endings

5. What *person and number* is the verb ἐλύομεν?
   a) Second singular
   b) Third plural
   c) First plural
   d) Second plural

6. What *person and number* is the verb ἔλυες?
   a) Second singular
   b) Third plural
   c) First plural
   d) Second plural

7. What *person and number* is the verb ἐλύεσθε?
   a) Second singular
   b) First singular
   c) First plural
   d) Second plural

8. The augment for a compound verb is:
   a) Placed at the beginning of the stem of the verb
   b) Placed after the preposition, before the stem of the verb
   c) Omitted because the verb is a compound
   d) Changed to an eta

9. Which of the following is NOT a part of a verb in the imperfect?
   a) Augment
   b) Past tense stem
   c) Connecting vowel
   d) Secondary active personal endings

10. If a verb begins with a vowel, the augment will be formed by:
    a) Omitting the augment
    b) Adding a consonant after the augment
    c) Lengthening the vowel
    d) Doubling the vowel

ANSWER KEY

1. C, 2. B, 3. A, 4. A, 5. C, 6. A, 7. D, 8. B, 9. B, 10. C

CHAPTER 22

Second Aorist Active and Middle Indicative

You Should Know

- What is the best translation for the word ἀποθνῄσκω?
  - I die, am about to die
- What is the best translation for the word πῦρ, -ός, τό?
  - Fire
- What is the best translation for the word ἄρτος, -ου, ὁ?
  - Bread
- What is the best translation for the word βάλλω?
  - I throw
- What is the best translation for the word προσεύχομαι?
  - I pray
- What is the best translation for the word γίνομαι?
  - I am, become, exist
- What is the best translation for the word εὑρίσκω?
  - I find
- What is the best translation for the word γῆ, γῆς, ἡ?
  - Earth, land
- The aorist indicates a perfective action usually occurring in the past. For now it should be translated with the simple undefined past tense in English.

- Greek has two ways to form the aorist. There is no difference in meaning between the two, only their form.

- If a word has a second aorist, the verbal root will usually have been changed in the formation of the present tense stem.

- The second aorist tense stem is usually the unmodified verbal root. This means the second aorist tense stem will usually have a different vowel or a consonantal change that differentiates it from the present.

- The second aorist active is formed by using an augment, second aorist active tense stem, connecting vowel, and secondary active endings.

- The second aorist middle is formed by using an augment, second aorist active tense stem, connecting vowel, and secondary middle/passive endings.

- The second aorist looks like the imperfect except that it uses the second aorist tense stem.

Quiz

1. An aorist verb describes:
    a) A perfective action which is usually in the present
    b) A completed action which is usually in the present
    c) A perfective action which is usually in the past
    d) An ongoing action which is usually in the past

2. An aorist verb is normally translated:
    a) With a continuous past, "I was studying"
    b) With the simple past, "I studied"
    c) As an undefined action, "I study"
    d) With a past-tense helping verb, "I had studied"

3. The second aorist active indicative is formed by:
    a) Augmenting the present active stem and adding secondary endings

Second Aorist Active and Middle Indicative | 81

  b) Augmenting the aorist active stem and adding primary endings
  c) Augmenting the aorist active stem and adding secondary endings
  d) Augmenting the present active and adding primary endings

4. What *person and number* is the verb ἔλαβον?
   a) Second singular
   b) Third plural
   c) First plural
   d) Second plural

5. What *person and number* is the verb ἐλάβετε?
   a) Second singular
   b) Third plural
   c) First plural
   d) Second plural

6. What *person and number* is the verb ἐγένετο?
   a) Second singular
   b) Third singular
   c) First plural
   d) Second plural

7. The aorist active tense form is listed as which number form of the verb in the lexicon?
   a) First
   b) Second
   c) Third
   d) Fourth

8. The word for "still" or "yet" is:
   a) ἔτι
   b) οὔτε
   c) λύω
   d) μᾶλλον

9. The word for "I take" or "receive" is:
   a) προσέρχομαι
   b) λαμβάνω

c) μᾶλλον
d) δεξιός

10. The word for "and not" or "neither" is:
    a) προσέρχομαι
    b) οὔτε
    c) λύω
    d) δεξιός

ANSWER KEY
1. C, 2. B, 3. C, 4. B, 5. D, 6. B, 7. C, 8. A, 9. B, 10. B

CHAPTER 23

First Aorist Active and Middle Indicative

You Should Know

- What is the best translation for the word ἀπέρχομαι?
  - I depart
- What is the best translation for the word κηρύσσω?
  - I proclaim
- What is the best translation for the word ἄρχομαι?
  - I begin
- What is the best translation for the word δοξάζω?
  - I glorify
- What is the best translation for the word γράφω?
  - I write
- What is the best translation for the word διό?
  - Therefore, for this reason
- What is the best translation for the word δύναμις, -εως, ἡ?
  - Power, miracle
- Like the second aorist, the first aorist (perfective) describes an undefined action usually occurring in past time.
- A verb that has a first aorist stem forms its aorist active by adding an augment, tense formative (σα), and secondary personal endings to the aorist active tense stem, which is usually the same as the present tense stem and its verbal root.

- The aorist middle is formed in the same way as is the active except that it uses middle/passive personal endings.
- Contract verbs lengthen their final stem vowel before the tense formative.
- Verbs with stems ending in a stop behave in the aorist as they do in the future in reference to the σ of the tense formative.
- Liquid aorists use α and not σα as their tense formative, and sometimes modify their tense stem.

Quiz

1. A first aorist verb is formed by:
    a) Augmenting the present active stem and adding secondary active personal endings
    b) Augmenting the aorist active stem and adding the tense sign σα and secondary active personal endings
    c) Augmenting the aorist active stem and adding secondary endings
    d) Augmenting the aorist active and adding the tense sign θη and secondary active personal endings

2. What *person and number* is the verb ἐλύσαμεν?
    a) Second singular
    b) Third plural
    c) First plural
    d) Second plural

3. What *person and number* is the verb ἐλύσατε?
    a) Second singular
    b) Third plural
    c) First plural
    d) Second plural

4. What *person and number* is the verb ἐλυσάμεθα?

a) Second singular
   b) Third plural
   c) First plural
   d) Third singular

5. What *person and number* is the ver: ἐλύσαντο?

   a) Second singular
   b) Third plural
   c) First plural
   d) First singular

6. Which of the following is the proper first aorist form of βλέπω?

   a) βλέψας
   b) ἔβλεψα
   c) βλέπων
   d) ἔβλεπον

7. First aorist stems ending in a labial form which of the following when joined to the tense formative?

   a) σ
   b) ξ
   c) ψ
   d) None of the above

8. First aorist active stems ending in a dental:

   a) Lose the dental
   b) Need a connecting vowel
   c) Form a ψ
   d) Form a ξ

9. Which of the following stems modify regularly in verbal root pattern 4?

   a) *γραφ
   b) *ἐλευθ
   c) *διδακ
   d) *δοξαδ

10. Which of the following stems are liquid stems following verbal root pattern 3?
   a) *βαπτιδ
   b) *κηρυγ
   c) *ἀποστελ
   d) *λεγ

ANSWER KEY

1. B, 2. C, 3. D, 4. C, 5. B, 6. B, 7. C, 8. A, 9. D, 10. C

CHAPTER 24

Aorist and Future Passive Indicative

You Should Know

- What is the best translation for the word φοβέομαι?
  - I fear
- What is the best translation for the word ἄγω?
  - I lead, bring
- What is the best translation for the word ὑπάγω?
  - I depart
- What is the best translation for the word αἷμα, -τος, τό?
  - Blood
- What is the best translation for the word ἱμάτιον, -ου, τό?
  - Garment
- What is the best translation for the word ἕκαστος, -η, -ον?
  - Each, every
- What is the best translation for the word ὄρος, -ους, τό?
  - Mountain, hill
- What is the best translation for the word χαίρω?
  - I rejoice
- The aorist and future passives are formed from the same tense stem. It is listed sixth and last in the lexical entry.
- The aorist passive is formed with an augment, the aorist passive tense stem, tense formative (θη or η), and secondary active endings.

- The future passive is formed with the aorist passive tense stem (no augment), tense formative (θησ or ησ), connecting vowel, and primary passive endings.
- Both the aorist passive and future passive are perfective in aspect.
- Your teacher will decide if you are to learn that some verbs are aorist passive deponent, or else that θη forms overlap with the σα forms and that by default θη forms are translated as passive but can also be middle.

Quiz

1. The first aorist passive verb is formed by:
   a) Augmenting the present active stem and adding primary personal endings
   b) Augmenting the aorist passive stem and adding the tense formative θη and secondary active personal endings
   c) The aorist active (no augment), adding the tense sign θη and secondary personal endings
   d) Augmenting the imperfect active and adding the tense sign θη

2. The tense sign for the future passive is:
   a) θη
   b) θησ
   c) σ
   d) σα

3. What is the tense formative for the second aorist passive?
   a) θη
   b) η
   c) θησ
   d) ησ

4. What is the tense formative for the first aorist passive?
   a) θη
   b) η
   c) θησ
   d) ησ

Aorist and Future Passive Indicative | 89

5. As a basic rule, you can translate aorist middle forms as:
   a) Passive
   b) Active
   c) Deponent
   d) None of the above

6. The aorist and future passive tense forms are listed as which number form of the verb in the lexicon?
   a) First
   b) Third
   c) Fourth
   d) Sixth (or last)

7. What *person and number* is the verb ἐλύθη?
   a) Second singular
   b) Third singular
   c) First plural
   d) Second plural

8. What *person and number* is the verb ἐλύθητε?
   a) Third singular
   b) First singular
   c) First plural
   d) Second plural

9. Identify the verb ἐλύθημεν
   a) Aorist middle indicative, 1P
   b) Future middle indicative, 3P
   c) Aorist passive indicative, 1P
   d) Aorist passive indicative, 1S

10. Identify the verb ἐλύσασθε
    a) Aorist passive indicative, 2P
    b) Aorist middle indicative, 2P
    c) Future middle indicative, 3P
    d) Aorist passive indicative, 3P

ANSWER KEY
1. B, 2. B, 3. B, 4. A, 5. B, 6. D, 7. B, 8. D, 9. C, 10. B

CHAPTER 25

Perfect Indicative

You Should Know

- What is the best translation for the word μαρτυρέω?
  - I bear witness, testify
- What is the best translation for the word μᾶλλον?
  - More, rather
- What is the best translation for the word αἰτέω?
  - I ask, demand
- The word for "I depart" is:
  - ὑπάγω
- The word for "I glorify" is:
  - δοξάζω
- The perfect tense indicates a completed action whose effects are felt in the speaker's present (combinative).
- The perfect active is formed with reduplication, the perfect active tense stem, tense formative (κα), and primary active personal endings.
- The perfect middle/passive is formed with reduplication, the perfect middle/passive tense stem, and primary middle/passive personal endings. There is no tense formative or connecting vowel.
- Verbs that begin with a single consonant reduplicate the initial consonant and separate them with an ε. If the initial consonant is φ, χ, or θ, the reduplicated consonant will be π, κ, or τ, respectively.

- Verbs beginning with a consonant cluster or a vowel usually undergo a vocalic reduplication (lengthening). Initial diphthongs usually do not reduplicate.

- Compound verbs reduplicate the verbal part of the word.

- Contract verbs lengthen their contract vowel in both the perfect active and perfect middle/passive.

- Perfect tense verbs can be translated using "have/has" and the past participle, or with the present as warranted by the context.

Quiz

1. The Greek perfect tense describes:
   a) A simple past action
   b) An action brought to completion in the past
   c) An action brought to completion in the past and whose effects are felt in the present
   d) A punctiliar action in the past

2. The perfect active verb is formed by:
   a) Augmenting the aorist active stem and adding the tense sign κα
   b) Reduplicating the initial consonant and adding the tense sign σα
   c) Reduplicating the initial consonant of the verb and adding the tense sign κα
   d) Augmenting the imperfect active and adding the tense sign κα

3. Which of the following is NOT a part of the perfect active verb?
   a) Perfect active tense stem
   b) Passive middle tense stem
   c) Primary active personal endings
   d) None of the above

4. In Greek, the perfect tense is often used to:
   a) Give a simple prediction
   b) Denote casual speech

c) Express great theological truths
d) Give a command
e) All of the above

5. Which of the following is an example of a statement using the Greek perfect?

   a) "Jesus died"
   b) "Jesus has died"
   c) "It stands written"
   d) All of the above
   e) None of the above
   f) B & C

6. What *person and number* is the verb λελύκατε?

   a) Second singular
   b) Third singular
   c) First plural
   d) Second plural

7. What *person and number* is the verb λέλυται?

   a) Second singular
   b) Third singular
   c) First plural
   d) Third plural

8. Identify the verb λέλυσαι

   a) Perfect middle indicative, 2S
   b) Perfect middle indicative, 1P
   c) Perfect active indicative, 3P
   d) Aorist passive indicative, 1P

9. What is the most notable difference in form between the perfect and other tenses?

   a) Reduplication
   b) The connecting vowel is in the beginning
   c) No tense formation
   d) The presence of θησ

10. The Greek pluperfect tense describes:
    a) A simple past action
    b) An action brought to completion in the past and whose effects are not yet felt
    c) An action brought to completion in the past and whose effects are felt in the present
    d) An action brought to completion in the past and whose effects are felt after completion but before the time of the speaker

ANSWER KEY
1. C, 2. C, 3. B, 4. C, 5. F, 6. D, 7. B, 8. A, 9. A, 10. D

CHAPTER 26

Introduction to Participles

You Should Know

- The *imperfective* active participle uses the morpheme:
  - ντ
- The *perfective* active participle uses the morpheme:
  - ντ
- The *combinative* active participle uses the morpheme:
  - οτ
- The word is used to negate most participles:
  - μή
- The tense stem and aspect of the *imperfective* participle:
  - Continuous action and present tense stem
- The tense stem and aspect of the *perfective* participle:
  - Undefined action and aorist tense stem
- The tense stem and aspect of the *combinative* participle:
  - Completed action and perfect tense stem
- A participle is a verbal adjective, sharing characteristics of both a verb and an adjective.
- As a verb, it has tense (present, aorist, perfect) and voice (active, middle, passive).
- As an adjective, it agrees with the word it modifies in case, number, and gender.

Introduction to Participles | 95

- A participle can be adverbial, modifying a verbal form (always anarthrous), or adjectival (usually articular).
- Participles do not indicate absolute time but rather aspect.
- The imperfective participle is built on the present tense stem and describes a continuous action.
- The perfective participle is built on the unaugmented aorist tense stem and describes an undefined action.
- The combinative participle is built on the perfect tense stem and describes a completed action with ongoing effects.

Quiz

1. In English, a participle is recognized by which of the following word endings?
    a) "-ed"
    b) "-ing"
    c) "-ly"
    d) "-s" or "-es"
    e) A & B
    f) B & D
    g) All of the above

2. The participle and its modifiers are called a:
    a) Gerund
    b) Relative clause
    c) Participial phrase
    d) Parenthetical statement

3. Which of the following is/are NOT part of the form of a participle?
    a) Tense stem of a verb
    b) Connecting vowel or tense formative
    c) Morpheme
    d) Case endings
    e) None of the above

4. The primary significance of a participle is its:

a) Tense
b) Voice
c) Aspect
d) Mood
e) None of the above

5. What determines the *tense* of a participle?
   a) The aspect conveyed
   b) Its relationship to the word it is modifying
   c) Its case endings
   d) The word it is modifying

6. What determines the *voice* of a participle?
   a) The aspect conveyed
   b) Its relationship to the word it is modifying
   c) Its case endings
   d) The word it is modifying

7. What determines the *case, number, and gender* of a participle?
   a) The aspect conveyed
   b) Its relationship to the word it is modifying
   c) Its case endings
   d) The word it is modifying

8. When a participle modifies a *verb*, it is usually translated:
   a) As a prepositional phrase
   b) As an adverbial phrase
   c) As a gerund
   d) As a separate sentence

9. When a participle modifies a *noun*, it is usually translated:
   a) As a gerund
   b) As a prepositional phrase
   c) As an adjectival phrase
   d) As a prepositional phrase

10. (T/F) If a participle modifies a noun, it agrees in person, number, and gender.

ANSWER KEY

1. B, 2. C, 3. E, 4. C, 5. A, 6. B, 7. D, 8. B, 9. C, 10. T

CHAPTER 27

Imperfective (Present) Adverbial Participles

You Should Know

- What is the best translation for the word τρεῖς, τρία?
  - Three
- What is the best translation for the word ἀναβαίνω?
  - I go up
- What is the best translation for the word πείθω?
  - I persuade
- What is the best translation for the word παρακαλέω?
  - I urge, encourage, comfort
- What is the best translation for the word ἀρχιερεύς, -έως, ὁ?
  - High priest
- What is the best translation for the word κάθημαι?
  - I sit (down)
- What is the best translation for the word θεωρέω?
  - I look at, behold
- What is the best translation for the word ἕτερος, -α, -ον?
  - Other, another, different
- What is the best translation for the word καταβαίνω?
  - I go (down)

- What is the best translation for the word εὐαγγελίζω?
  - I bring good news

- The imperfective participle is built on the present tense stem of the verb and indicates a continuous action. There is no absolute time significance to a participle.

- An adverbial participle describes an action that is related to the verb, and its form is determined by the word it modifies.

- The adverbial participle is always anarthrous.

- The participle of εἰμί looks like the participle morpheme with a case ending, always with smooth breathing.

- To translate you must first discover a participle's aspect, voice, and meaning. You can usually translate a present participle with the "-ing" form of the verb, sometimes with the key words "while" or "because."

- Memorize the Participle Morpheme Chart and the Master Participle Chart.

Quiz

1. An anarthrous participle:
    a) Always has a definite article
    b) Never has a definite article
    c) Is always adverbial
    d) Agrees with a noun with a definite article

2. Which of the following is NOT a morpheme for present participles?
    a) ντ
    b) ουσα
    c) μενο / μενη
    d) οτ
    e) None of the above

3. (T/F) The usual active morpheme for the present participle is θησ.

4. (T/F) The usual active morpheme for the present participle is μεν.

5. (T/F) Active participles use third declension endings.

6. (T/F) Middle/passive participles use third declension endings.

7. Identify λύων:
    a) Present middle/passive participle, masc nom sing
    b) Present active participle, masc nom sing
    c) Present active participle, fem nom sing
    d) Present active participle, neut nom sing

8. Identify λύοντι:
    a) Present middle/passive participle, masc nom sing
    b) Present active participle, masc nom sing
    c) Present active participle, neut dat sing
    d) Present middle/passive participle, fem nom pl

9. Identify λυομένων:
    a) Present middle/passive participle, masc nom pl
    b) Present active participle, masc nom sing
    c) Present middle/passive participle, fem gen pl
    d) Present middle/passive participle, masc dat sing

10. Identify λυομένοις:
    a) Present active participle, fem nom pl
    b) Present middle/passive participle, masc dat pl
    c) Present active participle, fem gen pl
    d) Present middle/passive participle, neut dat sing

ANSWER KEY
1. B, 2. D, 3. F, 4. F, 5. T, 6. F, 7. B, 8. C, 9. C, 10. B

CHAPTER 28

Perfective (Aorist) Adverbial Participles

You Should Know

- What is the best translation for the word σπείρω?
  - I sow

- What is the best translation for the word ἀσπάζομαι?
  - I greet, salute

- What is the best translation for the word κράζω?
  - I cry out

- What is the best translation for the word γραμματεύς, -έως, ὁ?
  - Scribe

- What is the best translation for the word ἱερόν, -οῦ, τό?
  - Temple

- What is the best translation for the word παιδίον, -ου, τό?
  - Child, infant

- What is the best translation for the word οὐχί?
  - Not

- The perfective participle is formed from the unaugmented aorist tense stem and indicates an undefined action.

- The perfective participle (first aorist) is formed from the unaugmented aorist tense stem + tense formative + participle morpheme + case endings.

Perfective (Aorist) Adverbial Participles | 101

- The perfective participle describes an undefined action; it does not describe a past event.
- You can use "after" in your translation of this participle.
- If a verb has a second aorist, the perfective participle of that verb will use the second aorist tense stem. Because it is second aorist, it uses a connecting vowel and not a tense formative.

Quiz

1. Which of the following is NOT part of the formation of the perfective participle (first aorist)?
   a) Unaugmented first aorist tense stem
   b) Tense formation
   c) Connecting vowel
   d) Participle morpheme
   e) Case ending

2. Which of the following is NOT part of the formation of the perfective active participle (second aorist)?
   a) Unaugmented second aorist tense stem
   b) Tense formation
   c) Connecting vowel
   d) Participle morpheme
   e) Case ending

3. Which of the following is true for perfective passive participles?
   a) The passive participle morpheme is ντ
   b) The η in the tense formative (θη) shortens to ε (θε)
   c) In the feminine the ντ has been replaced by ισα
   d) All of the above

4. Identify λύσαντες:
   a) Aorist active participle, masc nom plural
   b) Present active participle, masc nom sing
   c) Aorist active participle, fem nom sing
   d) Aorist middle participle, masc nom plural

5. Identify λυσαμένου:
   a) Aorist active participle, masc nom plural
   b) Aorist middle participle, masc gen sing
   c) Present active participle, neut nom sing
   d) Aorist active participle, masc gen plural

6. Identify λυθέντος:
   a) Aorist passive participle, masc nom plural
   b) Aorist middle participle, masc gen sing
   c) Present passive participle, neut nom sing
   d) Aorist passive participle, masc gen sing

7. Identify βαλλόμενα:
   a) Aorist middle participle, masc dat plural
   b) Aorist passive participle, masc acc sing
   c) Present middle/passive participle, neut nom plural
   d) Aorist passive participle, masc gen sing

8. Identify βαλοῦσα:
   a) Aorist middle participle, masc gen sing
   b) Aorist active participle, fem nom sing
   c) Aorist passive participle, neut nom plural
   d) Aorist passive participle, fem dat plural

9. The word for "so that" is:
   a) δεξιός
   b) μαρτυρέω
   c) ὥστε
   d) αἰτέω

10. The word for "more" is:
    a) αἰτέω
    b) μαρτυρέω
    c) μᾶλλον
    d) λύω

ANSWER KEY

1. C, 2. B, 3. D, 4. A, 5. B, 6. D, 7. C, 8. B, 9. C, 10. C

CHAPTER 29

Adjectival Participles

You Should Know

- What is the best translation for the word φέρω?
  - I carry, bear
- What is the best translation for the word δέχομαι?
  - I take, receive
- What is the best translation for the word δοκέω?
  - I think, seem
- What is the best translation for the word πέμπω?
  - I send
- What is the best translation for the word ἐσθίω?
  - I eat
- The word for "I sit" is:
  - κάθημαι
- The word for "I find" is:
  - εὑρίσκω
- The word for "I cry out" is:
  - κράζω
- An adverbial participle agrees with a noun or pronoun in the sentence, but the action described by the participle is directed toward the verb. It is always anarthrous, and often will need to be translated with the key words *while* or *after*.

- An adjectival participle modifies a noun or pronoun, or functions like a noun. It is usually articular.

- If an adjectival participle is attributing something to a noun or pronoun, it is called an attributive participle. For the time being, the simple "-ing" form of the English verb is sufficient for translation. The participle will agree in case, number, and gender with the word it is modifying.

- If an adjectival participle is functioning as a noun, it is called a substantival participle. You will usually insert extra words into your translation to make sense of this construction. Use those words that enable you to repeat in English the true significance of the participle in Greek. Its case is determined by its function, its gender and number by the word it is replacing.

- Seven Questions to Ask of Any Participle You Meet:
    - Is the participle anarthrous (probably adverbial) or articular (adjectival)?
    - What word is the participle modifying (determined by its case, number, and gender)?
    - If it is adverbial, do you use "while" or "after"? If it is adjectival, is it attributive or substantival?
    - Does the participle modify a word or perform a function?
    - What is the aspect of the participle?
    - What is the voice of the participle?
    - What does the verb mean?

Quiz

1. If a participle is used attributively, it will:
    a) Agree in gender and number with the noun it modifies, but not the case
    b) Agree in gender, number, and case with the noun it modifies
    c) Never have a definite article

Adjectival Participles | 105

   d) Agree in case with the noun it modifies, but not in gender and number

2. A substantival participle:
   a) Functions like an adverb
   b) Will never have a definite article
   c) Functions like a noun
   d) Functions like an adjective

3. One of the best clues in determining if a participle is adjectival rather than adverbial is:
   a) The presence of a definite article
   b) If an adjective is present and there is nothing to modify
   c) The presence of a "to be" verb
   d) The lack of another adjective in the sentence

4. How can you tell if a participle is being used substantivally?
   a) If an adjective is present and there is nothing to modify
   b) The presence of a "to be" verb
   c) The lack of another adjective in the sentence
   d) The presence of a definite article

5. Which of the following keywords is/are NOT used with adjectival participles?
   a) "While"
   b) "After"
   c) "Because"
   d) "Which"
   e) All of the above

6. Which of the following keywords is/are used with adjectival participles?
   a) "That"
   b) "Those"
   c) "Who"
   d) All of the above
   e) None of the above

7. When translating a substantive participle, try adding the words:
   a) "By" or "with"
   b) "The one who" or "Those who"
   c) "While"
   d) "After"

8. If a participle is adverbial, when would you translate "after"?
   a) If the participle is present
   b) If the participle is aorist
   c) If the participle is perfect
   d) If the participle is anarthorus

9. What is the meaning of the name *Christopher* (Χρίστοφερ)?
   a) Sending Christ
   b) Asking Christ
   c) Bearing Christ
   d) Following Christ

10. The perfective and imperfective participles have a relative time significance:
    a) Only if they are adverbial
    b) Only if they are adjectival
    c) Regardless of whether they are adverbial or adjectival
    d) In no instance

ANSWER KEY

1. B, 2. C, 3. A, 4. A, 5. D, 6. D, 7. B, 8. B, 9. C, 10. C

CHAPTER 30

Combinative (Perfect) Participles and Genitive Absolutes

You Should Know

- What is the best translation for the word πρεσβύτερος, -α, -ον?
  - Elder, older

- What is the best translation for the word μηδέ?
  - And not

- The word for "I call" (to one's side) is:
  - παρακαλέω

- The word for "I go up" is:
  - ἀναβαίνω

- The word for "then" is:
  - τότε

- The word for "therefore" is:
  - διό

- The participle is a *verbal adjective*. It can function adverbially or adjectivally (attributive; substantive).

- If the participle is used *adverbially*, its form will agree with the noun or pronoun that is doing the action of the participle, normally the subject of the verb. It is *always* anarthrous.

- Adverbial participles are often translated as a *temporal clause* ("while," "after"), but can also use the key words "because," "by," "though," or can be translated as a finite verb.

- If the participle is used as an *attributive* adjective, it will agree with the word it modifies in case, number, and gender. It is *usually* articular.

- If the participle is used as a *substantive*, its case is determined by its function in the sentence, while its number and gender are determined by the word to which it refers. You will most likely add words in your translation based on natural gender.

- Because the participle does not indicate absolute time, the perfective participle is unaugmented. The combinative participle, however, does not lose its vocalic reduplication.

Quiz

1. What is the active morpheme for the perfect?
    a) θησ
    b) οντ
    c) κοτ
    d) μεν

2. The combinative participle indicates:
    a) A completed action that has consequences in the speaker's present
    b) A continuous action that has no effect on time
    c) A future action that has consequences in the speaker's present
    d) A past action that has consequences in the reader's present

3. Which of the following is/are a possible key word for translating participles?
    a) "By"
    b) "Though"

c) "While"
d) "Because"
e) All of the above
f) A & B

4. If a participle is used as a noun, its case is determined by:

    a) The substantival participle's function in the sentence
    b) Who or what the participle is representing
    c) The verb the participle is modifying
    d) The context of the rest of the sentence

5. If a participle is used as a noun, its number is determined by:

    a) The substantival participle's function in the sentence
    b) Who or what the participle is representing
    c) The verb the participle is modifying
    d) The context of the rest of the sentence

6. If a participle is used as a noun, gender is determined by:

    a) The substantival participle's function in the sentence
    b) Who or what the participle is representing
    c) The verb the participle is modifying
    d) The context of the rest of the sentence

7. Identify λελυμένον:

    a) Perfect active participle, masc nom sing
    b) Aorist middle/passive participle, fem nom sing
    c) Perfect middle/passive participle, masc acc sing
    d) Perfect active participle, neut dat sing

8. Identify λυσάμενη:

    a) Perfect active participle, fem nom sing
    b) Aorist middle participle, fem dat sing
    c) Perfect middle/passive participle, masc gen sing
    d) Aorist active participle, fem dat sing

9. Identify λελυκότα:

    a) Perfect active participle, neut nom plural
    b) Aorist active participle, fem dat sing

c) Perfect active participle, masc dat sing
d) Aorist active participle, masc gen sing

10. What is a genitive absolute?
    a) A noun or pronoun and a participle that are dependent on the main verb of the sentence
    b) A noun or pronoun and a participle that are not grammatically connected to the rest of the sentence
    c) A noun or pronoun and a participle that are in the imperative tense (a command)
    d) A noun or pronoun and a participle that are marked with several definite articles

ANSWER KEY
1. C, 2. A, 3. E, 4. A, 5. B, 6. B, 7. C, 8. B, 9. A, 10. B

CHAPTER 31

Subjunctive

You Should Know

- What is the best translation for the word λίθος, -ου, ὁ?
  - Stone

- What is the best translation for the word τοιοῦτος, -αύτη, -οῦτον?
  - Such, of such a kind

- The word for "someone" is:
  - τις

- The word for "only" is:
  - μόνος

- The word for "hour" is:
  - ὥρα

- The word for "man" is:
  - ἀνήρ

- The word for "until" is:
  - ἕως

- The subjunctive mood is used when a verb expresses a possibility, probability, exhortation, or axiomatic concept.

- A verb in the subjunctive has no time significance. Its only significance is one of aspect. The subjunctive built on the present tense stem indicates a continuous action (imperfective). The subjunctive built on the unaugmented aorist tense stem indicates an undefined action (perfective).

- The primary sign of the subjunctive is the lengthened connecting vowel. The endings are exactly the same in the aorist as in the present (primary endings).

- The "present general" is stating a general, axiomatic truth.

- Three signs of the subjunctive: following ἵνα, ἐάν, and other words formed with ἄν; lengthened connecting vowel (ω/η); no augment in the aorist

- The "future more probable" condition says that if something might happen, then something else will definitely happen. The speaker is thinking of a specific event in the future.

- μή is used to negate the nonindicative moods.

- The subjunctive is used in a hortatory comment (to which you add the helping phrase "let us") and in deliberative questions.

Quiz

1. The indicative mood is used to:
   a) Make a suggestion to the object of the verb
   b) Describe a potential event
   c) Make a statement about reality
   d) To ask a hypothetical question

2. The subjective mood is used to:
   a) Express a fact
   b) Suggest a possibility
   c) Demand a response
   d) Express wishful thinking

3. The combinative subjunctive occurs only ten times in the New Testament, all as forms of:
   a) οἶδα
   b) μή
   c) οὐ
   d) ἐάν

4. What kind of action is described by the subjunctive in the present and aorist tenses?
   a) Present tense
   b) Imperfective
   c) Aorist tense
   d) Perfective

5. Which of the following is NOT part of a present subjunctive verb?
   a) Present tense stem
   b) Tense formative
   c) Lengthened connecting vowel
   d) Primary personal endings

6. Identify λύσηται:
   a) Aorist middle/passive subjunctive, 2P
   b) Aorist middle subjunctive, 3S
   c) Present active subjunctive, 2S
   d) Perfect active subjunctive, 3S

7. Identify ποιῶμεν:
   a) Present middle/passive subjunctive, 1P
   b) Perfect active subjunctive, 3P
   c) Present active subjunctive, 1P
   d) Perfect middle/passive subjunctive, 3S

8. When a subjunctive is used to express purpose, it almost always follows:
   a) ὅτι
   b) ἵνα
   c) ἐάν
   d) ὅταν

9. When a subjunctive is used in a conditional statement, it almost always follows:
   a) ὅτι
   b) ἵνα
   c) ἐάν
   d) ὅταν

10. When a subjunctive is used in the first person to express an exhortation, it is called:
    a) Hortatory subjunctive
    b) Epexegetical subjunctive
    c) Deliberative subjunctive
    d) Homiletical subjunctive

ANSWER KEY

1. C, 2. B, 3. A, 4. B, 5. B, 6. B, 7. C, 8. B, 9. C, 10. A

CHAPTER 32

Infinitive

You Should Know

- What is the best translation for the word μέλλω?
  - I am about to

- What is the best translation for the word δίκαιος, -α, -ον?
  - Right, righteous, just

- The word for "I send" is:
  - πέμπω

- The word for "scribe" is:
  - γραμματεύς

- The word for "whoever" is:
  - ὅστις

- The word for "I wish" is:
  - θέλω

- The Greek infinitive is a verbal noun. It is not declined, although it is considered singular neuter and any accompanying article will be declined.

- The infinitive has no time significance, only aspect. The imperfective infinitive is built on the present tense stem and indicates a continuous action. The perfective infinitive is built on the unaugmented aorist tense stem and indicates an undefined action. The combinative infinitive is built on the perfect tense stem and indicates a completed action with ongoing effects.

- Technically an infinitive does not have a subject, but there will often be a word in the accusative functioning as if it were the subject.

- There are six main ways in which an infinitive is used: substantive; complementary infinitive; articular infinitive preceded by a preposition; purpose; result, expressed by ὥστε with the infinitive; indirect discourse.

Quiz

1. The noun that acts as the "subject" of an infinitive is in the:
   a) Accusative case
   b) Nominative case
   c) Vocative case
   d) Genitive case
   e) Dative case

2. The infinitive does NOT occur in which of the following tenses?
   a) Present
   b) Aorist
   c) Perfect
   d) Future
   e) None of the above

3. Identify λύεσθαι:
   a) Perfect middle/passive infinitive
   b) Aorist active infinitive
   c) Present active infinitive
   d) Present middle/passive infinitive

4. Identify λῦσαι:
   a) Perfect active infinitive
   b) Present middle/passive infinitive
   c) Aorist active infinitive
   d) Present active infinitive

5. Identify λυθῆναι:
   a) Perfect active infinitive
   b) Aorist passive infinitive

c) Present middle/passive infinitive
d) Aorist active infinitive

6. Infinitives preceded by articles are called:
   a) Anarthorus infinitive
   b) Particular infinitive
   c) Articular infinitive
   d) Definite infinitive

7. An infinitive which is used with a finite verb with an incomplete meaning is called a:
   a) Finite infinitive
   b) Complementary infinitive
   c) Epexegetical infinitive
   d) Articular infinitive

8. If an infinitive is preceded by the preposition εἰς it indicates:
   a) Reason for the action ("because")
   b) Time of the action ("when")
   c) Purpose of the action ("in order that")
   d) Result of the action ("so that")

9. If an infinitive is preceded by the preposition διά it indicates:
   a) Reason for the action ("because")
   b) Time of the action ("when")
   c) Purpose of the action ("in order that")
   d) Result of the action ("so that")

10. If an infinitive is preceded by the preposition ὥστε it indicates:
    a) Reason for the action ("because")
    b) Time of the action ("when")
    c) Purpose of the action ("in order that")
    d) Result of the action ("so that")

ANSWER KEY
1. A, 2. D, 3. D, 4. C, 5. B, 6. C, 7. B, 8. C, 9. A, 10. D

CHAPTER 33

Imperative

You Should Know

- What is the best translation for the word ἀπολύω?
  - I release

- What is the best translation for the word ἀπόλλυμι?
  - I destroy

- What is the best translation for the word εἴτε?
  - If, whether

- The word for "child" is:
  - παιδίον

- The word for "tongue" is:
  - γλῶσσα

- The word for "fruit" is:
  - καρπός

- The word for "law" is:
  - νόμος

- The word for "I follow" is:
  - ἀκολουθέω

- The imperative is the form of the verb used for commands and entreaties.

- It occurs in the second person (like English) and the third (in which case you use the key word "let" and supply a pronoun).

- The imperfective imperative built on the present tense stem indicates a continuous action. The perfective imperative built on the unaugmented aorist tense stem indicates an undefined action. There is no time significance with the imperative.

- The difference between aspect is difficult to carry over into English. You can use "continue" in the translation of the imperfective.

- There are three different kinds of prohibitions using the indicative, imperative, and subjunctive: οὐ with the future indicative; μή plus the present imperative. Prohibits a continuous action; μή plus the aorist imperative. Prohibits an undefined action.

- There are two ways to strengthen a negation with the subjunctive: μή plus the aorist subjunctive. "No!"; οὐ μή plus the aorist subjunctive. "This will certainly not occur!"

Quiz

1. An imperative is used for:
    a) Direct address
    b) Wishful Thinking
    c) A command
    d) Subtle encouragement

2. Which of the following is the best example of the translation of an imperative?
    a) "You should study"
    b) "Study!"
    c) "You ought to study"
    d) "Would that you study!"

3. What is the difference in time significance between the present and the aorist imperative?
    a) The imperative does not indicate time
    b) The present does not indicate time
    c) There is no difference between the two—both do not indicate time
    d) There is no difference between the two—both indicate time

4. Which of the following is/are an example of a combinative imperative formed from the perfect tense stem?
   a) πεφίμωσο
   b) ἔρρωσθε
   c) ἴστε
   d) All of the above

5. Which form(s) of the imperative seem to be irregular?
   a) Second person singular
   b) Third person singular
   c) Second person plural
   d) Third person plural
   e) A & B
   f) C & D

6. Why did Paul lose much of his influence in Corinth in the letters to the Corinthians?
   a) His opponents had grown stronger
   b) He was trying to run the church from afar
   c) He used too many strong imperatives
   d) All of the above
   e) A & B

7. Identify λυέτω:
   a) Present active imperative, 2S
   b) Present middle/passive imperative, 3P
   c) Present active imperative, 3S
   d) Aorist active infinitive, 3S

8. Identify λύεσθε:
   a) Present middle/passive imperative, 2P
   b) Present active imperative, 3P
   c) Present active imperative, 3S
   d) Aorist active infinitive, 2P

9. Identify λύσατε:
   a) Present active imperative, 2P
   b) Aorist active imperative, 2P

c) Aorist active imperative, 3S
   d) Aorist active infinitive, 3P

10. Identify λύθητε:
    a) Aorist active imperative, 2P
    b) Aorist active imperative, 3P
    c) Aorist passive imperative, 2P
    d) Present active infinitive, 3P

ANSWER KEY
1. C, 2. B, 3. A, 4. D, 5. A, 6. E, 7. C, 8. A, 9. B, 10. C

CHAPTER 34

Indicative of δίδωμι

You Should Know

- What is the best translation for the word ὑπάρχω?
  - I am, exist
- What is the best translation for the word δίδωμι?
  - I give (out)
- What is the best translation for the word ἔθνος, -ους, τό?
  - Nation, Gentiles
- What is the best translation for the word πίπτω?
  - I fall
- What is the best translation for the word λοιπός, -ή, -όν?
  - Remaining, the rest
- What is the best translation for the word παραδίδωμι?
  - I entrust, hand over, betray
- The word for "I seem" is:
  - δοκέω
- The word for "I deliver" is:
  - παραδίδωμι
- The word for "mountain" is:
  - ὄρος
- μι verbs reduplicate their initial stem letter to form the present and separate the reduplicated consonant with an ι. It is essential that you memorize the root of a μι verb along with its lexical form.

- μι verbs do not ordinarily use a connecting vowel in the present indicative ("athematic").

- μι verbs employ three different personal endings in the present active indicative: δίδωμι; δίδωσι(ν); διδόασι(ν).

- The stem vowel of μι verbs can lengthen and shorten. It is not so important to know when this will happen, but merely to recognize that it does.

- Most of the μι verbs use κα for the tense formative in the aorist.

Quiz

1. The μι conjugation is sometimes called the:
   a) Thematic conjugation
   b) Consonantal conjugation
   c) Athematic conjugation
   d) Syntactical conjugation

2. μι verbs are classified by their:
   a) Connecting vowel
   b) Stem vowel
   c) Root form
   d) All of the above

3. (T/F) μι verbs employ three different personal endings in the present active indicative.

4. (T/F) Because of its verbal root, δώσω can only be one form: the perfect.

5. What is the difference in a μι verb between an aorist and a perfect?
   a) The perfect uses an epsilon to separate the reduplicated consonant, the aorist uses an augment
   b) The perfect uses an iota to separate the reduplicated consonant, the aorist uses an epsilon
   c) The aorist uses the tense sign σα, the perfect uses κα
   d) The perfect does not use a tense sign at all in a μι verb

6. The phenomenon of lengthening, shortening, or dropping stem vowels in the μι verbs is called:
   a) Ablaut
   b) Genitive
   c) Ablative
   d) Athematic

7. Identify the tense of δίδωμι:
   a) Present
   b) Future
   c) Aorist
   d) Perfect

8. Identify the tense of ἐδώκαμεν:
   a) Present
   b) Future
   c) Aorist
   d) Perfect

9. Identify the tense of δέδωκας:
   a) Present
   b) Future
   c) Aorist
   d) Perfect

10. Identify the tense of δέδωκε:
    a) Present
    b) Future
    c) Aorist
    d) Perfect

ANSWER KEY
1. C, 2. B, 3. T, 4. F, 5. A, 6. A, 7. A, 8. C, 9. D, 10. D

CHAPTER 35

Nonindicative of δίδωμι and Conditional Sentences

You Should Know

- What is the best translation for the word ἁμαρτάνω?
  - I sin

- What is the best translation for the word διακονέω?
  - I serve

- What is the best translation for the word φανερόω?
  - I reveal, make known

- What is the best translation for the word ἁγιάζω?
  - I consecrate, sanctify

- What is the best translation for the word ἀπαγγέλλω?
  - I report, tell

- What is the best translation for the word σωτήρ, -ῆρος, ὁ?
  - Savior, deliverer

- What is the best translation for the word δικαιόω?
  - I justify

- What is the best translation for the word φόβος, -ου, ὁ?
  - Fear, reverence

- The word for "beginning" is:
  - ἀρχή

- The word for "resurrection" is:
  - ἀνάστασις
- The nonindicative forms of μι verbs are even easier to identify than the indicative forms. In the subjunctive the reduplicated stem is the only difference between the present and the aorist.
- The nonindicative of δίδωμι is pretty straightforward. Just pay attention to its root.
- The imperatives are also easy to recognize. Remember that μι verbs do not use a thematic vowel, so the imperative morpheme is added directly to the verbal root.
- First class conditional sentences say that if something is true (and the truth is assumed for the sake of the argument), then such and such will occur. The protasis is introduced with εἰ and its verb is in the indicative.
- Second class conditional sentences say that if something were true (and the truth is assumed to be false for the sake of the argument), then such and such would happen. The protasis is introduced with εἰ and an indicative verb, and the apodosis will normally have ἄν and a verb in a secondary tense in the indicative.

Quiz

1. Identify the mood of δῶ:
   a) Indicative
   b) Imperative
   c) Subjunctive
   d) Infinitive

2. Identify the mood of διδότω:
   a) Indicative
   b) Imperative
   c) Subjunctive
   d) Infinitive

3. Identify the mood of δῶτε:
   a) Indicative
   b) Imperative
   c) Subjunctive
   d) Infinitive

4. Identify the mood of διδόναι:
   a) Indicative
   b) Imperative
   c) Subjunctive
   d) Infinitive

5. Identify the mood of δότε:
   a) Indicative
   b) Imperative
   c) Subjunctive
   d) Participle

6. Identify the mood of διδοῦσα:
   a) Indicative
   b) Imperative
   c) Subjunctive
   d) Participle

7. A first class conditional sentence:
   a) Expresses a contrary-to-fact-condition
   b) Says something that is true or is assumed true
   c) Says something that is not true, but is likely to be true in the future
   d) Expresses a hypothetical statement that is unlikely to ever be true

8. A second class conditional sentence:
   a) Expresses a contrary-to-fact-condition
   b) Says something that is true or is assumed true
   c) Says something that is not true, but is likely to be true in the future
   d) Expresses a hypothetical statement that is unlikely to ever be true

9. A protasis is:
    a) The "then" part of a conditional sentence
    b) The "if" part of a conditional sentence
    c) A conditional sentence that ought to be translated "since"
    d) A conditional sentence that does not use "if"

10. An apodosis is:
    a) A sentence which implies a conditional situation
    b) The "if" part of a conditional sentence
    c) The "then" part of a conditional sentence
    d) A conditional sentence that does not use "if"

ANSWER KEY
1. C, 2. B, 3. C, 4. D, 5. B, 6. D, 7. B, 8. A, 9. B, 10. C

CHAPTER 36

Ἵστημι, τίθημι, δείκνυμι, and Odds 'n Ends

You Should Know

- What is the best translation for the word ἴδιος, -α, -ον?
  – One's own

- What is the best translation for the word μέσος, -η, -ον?
  – Middle

- What is the best translation for the word ἀνοίγω?
  – I open

- What is the best translation for the word φημί?
  – I say, affirm

- The word for "I rise" is:
  – ἀνίστημι

- The word for "I let go" or "I forgive" is:
  – ἀφίημι

- The word for "I show" is:
  – δείκνυμι

- The word for "I fall" is:
  – πίπτω

- μι verbs with stem vowels in α (ἵστημι) and ε (τίθημι) behave just like μι verbs with stem vowels in ο (δίδωμι). δείκνυμι, however, is somewhat different and in many ways more like the thematic conjugation.

- The athematic conjugation was in the process of being lost in Koine Greek, and consequently some μι verbs have thematic forms.
- When the article is present, it emphasizes the identity of the word/phrase it modifies.
- The article can also function as a grammatical marker.
- When the article is not present, the quality of the substantive is emphasized.
- "Normal" word order is conjunction, verb, subject, object.

Quiz

1. Identify the root of τίθημι:
    a) *θε
    b) *θη
    c) *μι
    d) None of the above

2. Identify the root of ἀνίστημι:
    a) ἀνά + *ὀλ
    b) ἀνά + *στα
    c) ἀνί + σ
    d) ἀνί + μι

3. ὁ can function as:
    a) A personal, possessive, or relative pronoun
    b) A grammatical marker
    c) A transformer of a participle or adjective into a noun
    d) All of the above
    e) B & C

4. Identify the tense of τέθεικα:
    a) Present
    b) Aorist
    c) Perfect
    d) Future

5. Identify the lexical form of ἔστησα:
   a) δείκνυμι
   b) τίθημι
   c) ἵστημι
   d) στασιάζω

6. Identify the tense, voice, and mood of ἔστησαν:
   a) Present, active, indicative
   b) Aorist, active, indicative
   c) Aorist, middle, indicative
   d) Present, middle, indicative

7. Aphesis is:
   a) The gradual loss of an initial unaccented vowel
   b) A demonstrative pronoun
   c) When the reduplicated θ changes to τ in verbs like τίθημι
   d) Another name for the four classes of μι verbs

8. A deictic article is best translated:
   a) As a condition ("if")
   b) As a demonstrative pronoun ("that")
   c) As in inference ("since")
   d) As a reference to a unique thing ("the only")

9. A transitive verb:
   a) Is used only in conditional sentences
   b) Carries the force of an action to an object
   c) Does not normally have a direct object
   d) Always takes a predicate nominative

ANSWER KEY

1. A, 2. B, 3. D, 4. C, 5. C, 6. B, 7. A, 8. B, 9. B

Notes

CPSIA information can be obtained
at www.ICGtesting.com
Printed in the USA
LVHW031911271219
641902LV00002B/3/P